W9-BVY-621

The Boston Red Sox

By Donald Honig

FICTION

Sidewalk Caesar
Walk Like a Man
The Americans
Divide the Night
No Song to Sing
Judgment Night
The Love Thief
The Severith Style
Illusions
I Should Have Sold Petunias
The Last Great Season
Marching Home

NONFICTION

Baseball When the Grass Was Real
Baseball Between the Lines
The Man in the Dugout
The October Heroes
The Image of Their Greatness (with Lawrence Ritter)
The 100 Greatest Baseball Players of All Time (with Lawrence Ritter)
The Brooklyn Dodgers: An Illustrated Tribute
The New York Yankees: An Illustrated History
Baseball's 10 Greatest Teams
The Los Angeles Dodgers: The First Quarter Century
The National League: An Illustrated History
The American League: An Illustrated History
Baseball America
The New York Mets: The First Quarter Century
The World Series: An Illustrated History
Baseball in the '50s
The All-Star Game: An Illustrated History
Mays, Mantle, Snider: A Celebration
Baseball's Greatest First Basemen
Baseball's Greatest Pitchers
A Donald Honig Reader
Baseball in the '30s
The Power Hitters
Baseball: An Illustrated History of America's Game

The Boston Red Sox

An Illustrated History

Donald Honig

New York London Toronto Sydney Tokyo

PRENTICE HALL PRESS
15 Columbus Circle
New York, New York 10023

Library of Congress Cataloging-in-Publication Data

Honig, Donald.
The Boston Red Sox : an illustrated history / by Donald Honig.—1st Prentice Hall Press ed.
p. cm.
Includes index.
ISBN 0-13-080326-X : $24.95
1. Boston Red Sox (Baseball team)—History. I. Title.
GV875.B62H66 1990
796.357'64'0974461—dc20 89-32698
CIP

Designed by Michael J. Freeland

Manufactured in the United States of America

10 9 8 7 6 5 4 3 2 1

First Edition

For my daughter, Catherine

ACKNOWLEDGMENTS

I am deeply indebted to a number of people for their generous assistance in photo research and help in gathering the photographs reproduced in this book. Special thanks go to Michael P. Aronstein, president of Card Memorabilia Associates, Ltd., and his son Andrew for their spirited help, and to Patricia Kelly and her tireless colleagues at the National Baseball Hall of Fame and Museum at Cooperstown, New York.

Gratitude must also be expressed to Tom Heitz and Bill Dean, librarian and chief research assistant, respectively, of the National Baseball Hall of Fame and Museum, for sharing with the author their vast knowledge of baseball history.

A particular note of appreciation must go to Larry Cancro, marketing director of the Boston Red Sox, for his support and encouragement.

Also, for their advice and counsel, a word of thanks to the following: Stanley Honig, Lawrence Ritter, David Markson, Louis Kiefer, Mary E. Gallagher, Douglas Mulcahy, Bob Wood, and Thomas, James, and Michael Brookman.

Thanks to Dave Dunton of Prentice Hall Press for his help and to Paul Aron, a sterling editor, who made sure the author touched every base.

CONTENTS

INTRODUCTION

Jacques Barzun has written, "Whoever wants to know the heart and mind of America had better learn baseball." A slight rewording of that widely quoted insight might read, "Whoever wants to know the heart and mind of the baseball fan might do well to study the years and times of the Boston Red Sox." Here is a team that has both shaken the baseball heavens and ridden the tides of glory, and languished in the depths, and inflicted upon their faithful followers the keenest of disappointments. And, through all of this, their fans, unwavering true believers, have stood fast with hope and optimism and, upon occasion, forgiveness.

It has been said that the Red Sox are part of the patrimony of New England; generation after generation has inherited a fidelity to the cause of the men of Fenway, known throughout New England as "The Sox." The Red Sox are as much a part of that historic corner of the American nation as the mountains, lakes, and shoreline that so graphically characterize it.

The focal point of this devotion is Fenway Park, the small, old, oddly shaped home field of the Red Sox since 1912. Built for a game that feeds off of its own history, that follows a seamless course through the years, Fenway is an ideal place to watch the adventures of baseball, where one can sit comfortably with the shadows of Babe Ruth, Jimmie Foxx, Ted Williams, and all the other titans who have passed this way. Every Red Sox fan is a shareholder in that history, possesses an anchorage in that past, and holds a ticket to the future.

Through their long and unpredictable history the Red Sox have been many things: triumphant, exciting, and gallant, as well as frustrating and disappointing. Through all the personnel changes that baseball teams must necessarily undergo, they have never failed to exude a certain charm that is rare in any athletic endeavor. These are the qualities of the Boston Red Sox, one of the ongoing enchantments of New England.

— 1 —

Birth of a Tradition

There stands in the city of Boston a power plant known as Fenway Park. It generates excitement, tension, jubilation, dismay, exasperation, pride, heartbreak, and, above all, loyalty and a curious faith that seems to be renewed each year by the long, snow-bearded New England winter. New England has always had these winters, as well as its White and its Green mountains, its Atlantic-stormed coastline. New England has long had its Yale and its Harvard, its haunting Indian names, its deep history. Comparatively recent to that history, but in their way as compelling and resounding to New England sensibilities as any echo from the past, are the men and the events of Fenway Park, men who never age, though by now some of them are nearly a century old, men wondrously young in white uniforms with those six cabalistic letters across their chests: *RED SOX*.

The Boston Red Sox begin at Fenway Park and then by a process that is equal parts faith, history, and love reach out to all of New England and are probably the only entity that most singular corner of the nation can unite around and agree upon.

As hard as it may be for their partisans to believe today, there was indeed a time when the Boston Red Sox did not exist. This flaw in the national culture was finally corrected in 1901, thanks to a man named Byron Bancroft Johnson—known as Ban—who was the founder, chief architect, and long-time president of the American League.

In the late 1890s, Johnson was president of a structure called the Western Association, considered the strongest of the minor leagues. Johnson was an ambitious man, and it was his aspiration and his intention to turn his circuit into a major league.

Johnson was hatching his plans in an era when the American entrepreneur could dream as audaciously as he pleased; it was the era of the robber barons, and while his field was baseball and not industry, Johnson was as single-minded and tough and devious as any Rockefeller, Gould, Carnegie, or Vanderbilt.

(OPPOSITE PAGE) Ban Johnson.

There was just a single major league in operation at the time—the twelve-team National League. The National League had come into existence in 1876 and in the ensuing quarter century had seen several competing, self-proclaimed major leagues come and go, including the American Association, the Union Association, and the Players' League.

As the only major league, the National League was a monopoly and, like most monopolies, tended to be authoritarian and high-handed in its treatment of its employees. There was a $2,400 salary cap, irrespective of performance, and players could be fined or suspended arbitrarily. A player had to like it or leave it.

In 1900, the Western Association changed its name to the American League, and the implications of this were clear, for the circuit was no longer to be a regional confection—Johnson had placed clubs in several eastern cities, much to the indignation of the National League. The latter's reaction turned even more heated a year later, when Johnson declared his operation a major league. The charter members were Chicago, Detroit, Cleveland, and Milwaukee, in the west; Boston, Philadelphia, Baltimore, and Washington, in the east. (In 1902 St. Louis replaced Milwaukee, and in 1903 New York replaced Baltimore. Thereafter, the alignment remained stable until 1954, when the St. Louis Browns moved to Baltimore.)

Johnson was being extremely bold and confrontational—Boston, Philadelphia, and Chicago were also National League cities; and when St. Louis and New York joined the new league, the two majors were in head-to-head competition in five of their eight cities.

Boston was, of course, no stranger to big-league baseball, having been one of the National League's founding members in 1876. The club, known originally as the Red Stockings and later acquiring the nickname "Beaneaters," was, in fact, one of the league's more formidable franchises, winning pennants in 1877, 1878, 1883, 1891, 1892, 1893, 1897, and 1898. Through the years some of baseball's top players had plied their trade in

Boston, including pitchers John Clarkson and Kid Nichols, first baseman Dan Brouthers, third baseman Jimmy Collins, and outfielders Mike ("King") Kelly, Tommy McCarthy, and Hugh Duffy.

Jimmy Collins (1901–07). *(Courtesy NBL)*

Ban Johnson could call his league anything he wanted—major, minor, whatever—but without star ballplayers it would be strictly minor. A major league required ballplayers commensurate with such status, but they were not a commodity available on the shelves of a general store. They couldn't be grown, acquired through advertising, or imported. There was, in fact, only one place to get them—the National League.

The lure of the American League's fresh checkbooks dissolved old loyalties and created new ones. Many of the National League's premier stars were dazzled by salaries as high as $4,000 or $5,000 a year. (The average annual income in the country at the time was less than $700, with a workweek that averaged close to sixty hours.) Among the players who succumbed to the lure of American League money were such stars as Cy Young, Nap Lajoie, Wee Willie Keeler, Ed Delahanty, Sam Crawford, Jesse Burkett, Jimmy Collins. For several years there was chaos, with players jumping back and forth between the leagues because of lucrative offers, litigation or the threat of litigation, or judicial decisions, which sometimes varied from one state to the next.

The sniping and fist-shaking went on for several years, until the National League finally realized that the new league had come to stay and that further squabbling would be ruinous for everyone. Not only had the American League established itself as a credible rival, but in the cities where the two circuits were in direct competition the newcomers were outdrawing the older clubs by substantial margins.

Despite the fact that the Boston National League team had been in town since 1876 and had built a winning tradition—five pennants in the previous ten years—the city's new club immediately won the hearts, the affection, and the loyalty of the fans. Red Sox magic, that mysterious alchemy that links team and fan in a bonding tighter than any marriage or contract ever could, was evident from the very beginning. It was as if all New England had been waiting for the creation of this baseball team. The devotion of Red Sox fans became so strong—in some quarters fanatic—that Boston was soon to be known as "a Red Sox town," to the extent that the Boston Braves finally gave up, moving to Milwaukee in 1953 and ceding the turf to the Sox.

The Pilgrims, as the Red Sox were known in those early years, were fortunate in their first owner, Charles Somers, who had acquired considerable wealth through the agencies of shipping, coal, and lumber. Somers was in many respects Ban Johnson's financial angel: The Boston owner also held interests in three other teams (an arrangement that would be unthinkable today), lending money to help Connie Mack get started in Philadelphia and Charles Comiskey in Chicago.

Somers moved quickly to show Boston fans that he meant business. In March 1901, he raided the roster of Boston's National League club and came away with third baseman Jimmy Collins, an established star, a local hero, and by all accounts the top third baseman of the era. Until the coming of Pie Traynor in the 1920s, Jimmy was generally regarded as the game's greatest third baseman.

Although he was steady with the bat (a .294 lifetime average), Collins was most noted for his glovework. Because of the frequent employment of the bunt as an offensive weapon in those dead-ball days, third base was considered a crucial defensive position, and by general consensus Jimmy was far and away the best, with a particular talent for swooping in on bunts and getting his man at first base.

The Red Sox hired the thirty-one-year-old Collins not only to play third base but also to manage. Jimmy's rationale for jumping from one Boston employer to another was a timeless one: "I like to play baseball," he said, "but this is a business for me and I can't be governed by sentiment." Spoken in March 1901, these words have not lost their currency—not in dugouts, clubhouses, or front-office suites. If there is sentiment in baseball, one writer has written, it comes in exclusively through the turnstiles.

Collins said that for several years he had been asking his employers for a salary increase. "But I was put aside with one flimsy excuse or another." The Pilgrims signed him to a contract that called for around $4,000 a year, a considerable jump up from the National League's $2,400 ceiling.

Also from the Boston Beaneaters (they didn't become known as the Braves until 1912) came a slim, hard-hitting first baseman–outfielder named Buck Freeman, who became the first in the Red Sox' long line of power hitters, and outfielder Chick Stahl.

The new club gave itself instant credibility with these acquisitions, but then it scored an even greater coup by hijacking from the National League the man then regarded as the game's greatest pitcher, the man whose name today is associated with baseball's most prestigious pitching award—Cy Young.

Young had been pitching in the National League since 1890 and had been a consistent big winner: eight times with 25 wins or better, including three times with 32 or better. It was true that in that era it was common for pitchers to win more than 20 games a year (with all of his gaudy totals, Young had led in victories only once), but what made Cy unique was his durability; the Ohio farmboy must have had the constitution and stamina of an ox, pitching more than 300 innings a year for fifteen consecutive years. He leads all major-league pitchers in these lifetime categories: wins (511), games started (815), complete games (751), and innings pitched (7,356), baseball records that seem to possess the towering durability of redwoods.

Cy claimed he never had a sore arm, "even though I usually pitched with just two days' rest and sometimes just one. Oh, it would get tired sometimes, but that never bothered me." His repertory, he said, consisted of "a couple of good curveballs. One was an overhand pitch that broke sharply down, the other a

Cy Young (1901–08): 511 lifetime victories.

sidearm sweeper. I'd wheel on the batter so as to hide the pitch, and I had excellent control. And I had that fastball too. It was plenty fast. A whistler." Young, who died in 1955 at the age of eighty-eight, claimed he had been every bit as fast as Walter Johnson, Lefty Grove, and Bob Feller, the touchstones for high-speed deliveries in the first half of the century. Was Cy just an old man telling tales? Maybe. But when a man has won 511 games, you tend to believe what he tells you.

Lou Criger (1901–08), Cy Young's favorite catcher. *(Courtesy NBL)*

It was because of a lack of restrictions that Boston was able to add Cy to the roster. From 1890 to 1898 he had pitched for Cleveland. After the 1898 season, he had been switched to the St. Louis club, a transaction made possible by the fact that the same man, James Robison, owned both clubs. Cy did not like working in St. Louis, objecting particularly to the broiling summer heat. His two years in the city were unhappy ones, so when the offer came to pitch for Boston, the thirty-four-year-old ace opted for its preferable climate, which was made even more temperate by a $3,500 salary.

Along with Cy came his favorite catcher, Lou Criger, a man light of stick but evidently most able of mitt. For years, Criger

The Huntington Avenue Grounds during a game in June 1903. Note the sellout crowd ringing the outfield. *(Courtesy NBL)*

was the man Cy preferred to have receive his curves and "whistlers."

Some other notables on that first Boston team were second baseman Hobe Ferris, shortstop Freddy Parent, and pitcher George Winter.

George Winter (1901–08). He was a 16-game winner in 1901 and again in 1905.

It may come as a cultural revelation to some of today's Red Sox fans, but their team did not always ply its trade at Fenway Park. The professional ancestors of today's double-knit-clad, lavishly compensated heroes began playing in a park known as the Huntington Avenue Grounds, today the site of Northeastern University's indoor athletic building. The all-wood park had a seating capacity of around 7,000, with overflow crowds permitted to stand in the outfield behind ropes. (This was common practice in the dead-ball era, when extremely long fly balls were rarities. A ball hit into the outfield crowd was a ground-rule double.)

(LEFT)
Hobe Ferris (1901–07).

(RIGHT)
Freddy Parent (1901–07), Boston's first shortstop. (*Courtesy NBL*)

— 2 —

Early Success

As the American League launched its first season in 1901, hopes were high and prospects seemed favorable. There were, however, the usual skeptics and doomsayers who are in attendance at every new enterprise, and most of these were National League people. Arthur Soden, owner of the Boston Beaneaters, surveyed the competition and said confidently, "Only one club will survive this battle in Boston, and that will be the same old National League club." John T. Brush, president of the Cincinnati Reds, said, "They are minor-league teams playing in major-league cities. The public will know the difference." There was also an element of sour grapes concerning Cy Young, with disgruntled National League owners insisting that the great pitcher was over the hill and that he might perhaps be able to "squeeze out one year against minor-league competition."

The bleak forecasts quickly proved to be ill founded, and nowhere more conclusively than in Boston. Here, Jimmy Collins's hearty newcomers drew nearly 290,000 customers (to 146,000 for their long-established in-town rivals). In fact, during the fifty-two years the Red Sox and Braves competed in the city of Boston, only seven times did the National League club outdraw the American. Whatever mysterious elixir creates the charm and allure of the Boston Red Sox wove its enchantment from the very beginning; the team was like a live Christmas present to be unwrapped anew every day, all summer long.

That first season was in some ways a preview of many Red Sox seasons to follow—a summerlong challenge for the pennant, some solid hitting, but then a late-season decline and a respectable but disappointing second-place finish, four games behind the pennant-winning Chicago White Sox.

Buck Freeman led the team with a .339 batting average and 114 runs batted in and also hit 12 home runs, which was a sizable number in those days when the baseball barely had a pulse (the leader was Nap Lajoie with 14; Nap also rattled

(OPPOSITE PAGE) Buck Freeman (1901–07), Boston's first heavy hitter. (*Courtesy NBL*)

league pitching for a .422 average, still the American League's all-time high). Skipper Collins set a good example with a .332 average, while Chick Stahl finished at .309 and Freddy Parent at .306.

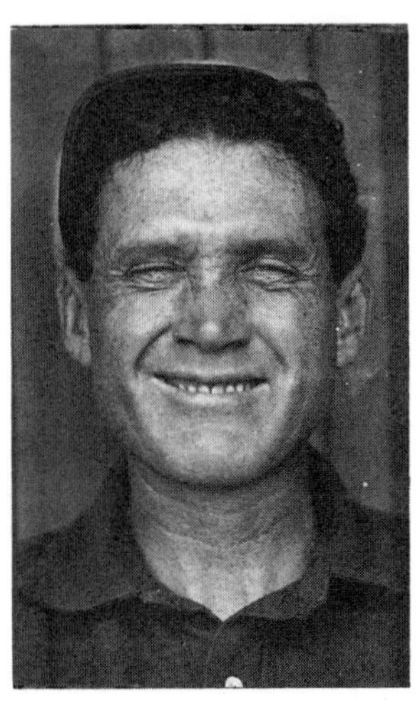

A .342 hitter in 1902, and a .331 hitter in 1903, Patsy Dougherty (1902–04) was a popular player in Boston's early years.

Cy Young, as ever, earned his money, the husky, tireless righthander racking up a 33–10 record, his win total more than double that of the team's next two starters, 16-game winners George Winter and Ted Lewis. If there had been a Cy Young Award in 1901, Cy Young would have won it easily. In addition to his superb won-lost record, the Boston ace led the league in earned run average (1.62), shutouts (5), and strikeouts (158). The big man also knew where his curves and "whistlers" were going: in 371 innings he walked just 37, or one every 10 innings. Making Cy's 33 wins even more impressive was the fact that the American League played a 138-game schedule that year. (The 154-game schedule went into effect in 1904.)

First baseman Candy LaChance (1902–05).

In 1902, the Pilgrims did some reshaping of the club. Buck Freeman, the team's first baseman and best hitter, was moved to the outfield to make room for George ("Candy") LaChance. One sportswriter described the removal of Freeman to the outfield as being "salubrious for the team's defense"—which tells us that Buck was not the smoothest of glovemen.

Patsy Dougherty was added to the outfield, and the genial young Irishman led the club with a .342 batting average. With Freeman at .309 (plus a league-high 121 RBIs) and Stahl at .323, the team had its first all-.300-hitting outfield.

The pitching was again Cy Young, who was 32–11 and was again the league's dominant pitcher. In addition to Cy, the club had right-hander Bill Dinneen, who had been lured away from the Boston National League club and who posted a break-even 21–21 record. Dinneen, who later umpired in the American League, had wanted to join the new club in 1901 but had been concerned about the league's survival.

"It was all right for Cy to jump," he said, "because if the league folded he wouldn't have any problem getting another job." This fear of being blackballed kept Dinneen with the Beaneaters in 1901, but when the new league's success became evident, he skipped out and enlisted with the Pilgrims.

With Young winning 32 and Dinneen 21, the club had a strong one-two punch on the mound, but after that the pitching thinned to near invisibility, with Winter's 11 wins next highest. This lack of front-line pitching landed the Pilgrims in third place, six and a half games behind Connie Mack's pennant-winning Philadelphia Athletics.

Bill Dinneen (1902–07), a three-time twenty-game winner for Boston.

Between them, Young and Dinneen started 85 of the team's 138 games, with Cy completing 41 of 43 starts and Bill 39 of 42. In those years, teams had seventeen-man rosters and consequently smaller pitching staffs than they do today. With the average staff consisting of five pitchers, starters were expected to go the distance; relief pitching as a specialty job was unknown. The eight American League pitching staffs in 1902 averaged approximately 120 complete games apiece. Pitchers worked more innings in those days—fifteen American League pitchers turned in more than 250 innings that year—but because of the dead ball, they did not have to work as hard pitch by pitch as they do today. There was little chance of a mistake being rocketed over the fence, which is today's penalty. Many of the home runs hit back then were inside the park, because the dead ball allowed outfielders to play shallow, which gave them less time to run down a ball hit into a gap. The "long ball" in those days was the triple, with most clubs hitting two or three times as many triples as home runs.

The ownership of the team changed hands after the close of the 1902 season, with Milwaukee attorney Henry Killilea buying out the interests of Charles Somers. Killilea was a friend of Ban Johnson's, which seems to have been almost a prerequisite for obtaining an American League franchise in those heady years.

The 1903 season remains one of the glory summers of Boston baseball history. The year began with a truce being reached

That's Hobe Ferris making the play at second for Boston. Note Hobe's glove. (*Courtesy NBL*)

between the warring leagues, with the important articles being an agreement to respect each other's players' contracts and to cease raiding rosters. The year also saw the placement of a New York franchise in the American League, a team destined to bear heavily upon Red Sox fortunes in the future.

Right-hander Tom Hughes (1902–03). He was a 20-game winner for Boston in 1903, then was traded to New York.

By the end of May, the Pilgrims were in first place, and there they remained for virtually the rest of the season, winning steadily, and finishing fourteen and a half games ahead of the runner-up Athletics.

Patsy Dougherty led the team with a .331 batting average and the league with 195 hits, and Buck Freeman led in RBIs (104) for the second straight year and also became Boston's first home-run king, with a total of 13. The club as a whole hit 48 home runs, which stood as the American League record until 1920, when the lively ball was introduced. The team also led in batting (.272), slugging (.392), triples (113—still the club record), hits (1,336), and runs (707).

This effective batting attack backed up a pitching staff that included three twenty-game winners: Young (28–9), Dinneen (21–13), and right-hander Tom Hughes, known as "Long Tom" (20–7). Hughes had been with the team in 1902 but been hampered by a sore arm. He had that one full, productive season with Boston and then was traded to New York for left-hander Jesse Tannehill. Young was the league leader in victories for the third year in a row. For his first three years in Boston, the mighty Cy (whose real name was Denton True Young) was 93–30, which is the way to go if you want to have an award named after you.

It was during the 1903 season that a new idea began brewing in baseball. The American League was vigorously out of its cradle now, had received grudging recognition from the National League, and was clearly here to stay; so it seemed natural to arrange a postseason match between the respective pennant winners to crown a champion of the universe of baseball.

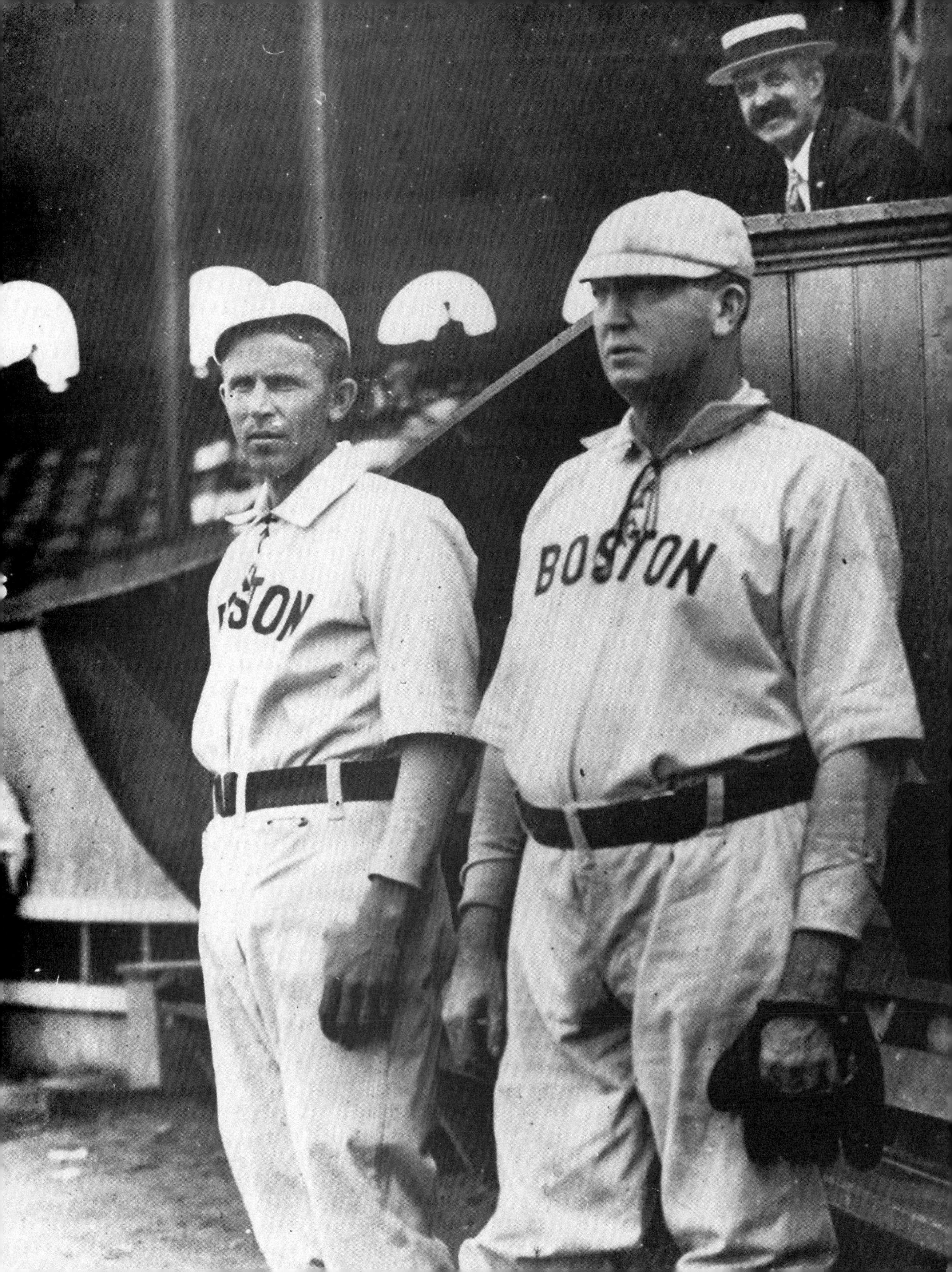
BOSTON

(Opposite page) Lou Criger (*left*) and Cy Young.

There were some hard-line National Leaguers—New York Giants manager John McGraw chief among them (McGraw had a strong personal dislike of Ban Johnson)—who were opposed to the idea of putting their players on the same field with the players of what they still sneeringly regarded as a "minor league." Nevertheless, there were others who saw such a match as a stimulant for their game as well as a sound business move.

Among the latter was the owner of the Pittsburgh Pirates, Barney Dreyfuss. Dreyfuss's club, then the power of the National League, was heading for a third straight pennant. Accordingly, the Pirates' owner wrote a letter in August to Henry Killilea, whose team was also on the high road to the pennant, suggesting their employees meet in a postseason series to determine baseball's best team.

Killilea liked the idea and took up the matter with Ban Johnson. The autocratic head of the American League immediately saw the possibilities and advantages of such a contest. (Who first uttered those now magical words "World Series" is not known.) The Series' very existence would give the younger league parity with the older, and an American League victory

A look into the Boston dugout during the 1903 World Series. Cy Young is at the far left, Candy LaChance on the near right.

would dispel any lingering vestiges of doubt about its equality. One thing, however, nagged at Johnson: the possibility of defeat.

"Play them," Killilea was told. "But you must beat them."

Killilea passed Johnson's injunction along to Collins and his men. The skipper knew that beating Pittsburgh would not come easily. Jimmy had, after all, been in the National League just a few years before and was familiar with the quality of some of the Pirate stars, notably pitchers Deacon Phillippe and Sam Leever, outfielder-manager Fred Clarke, outfielder Ginger Beaumont, and most especially the great shortstop Honus Wagner, in the opinion of many the mightiest player of the day.

It was decided to make the Series a nine-game affair, with the first team to win five taking the championship. (The World Series of 1919, 1920, and 1921 were played under this same format; every other Series has been a best-of-seven contest.) The first three games were scheduled to be played in Boston, the next four in Pittsburgh, and the final two, if necessary, in Boston.

Sensing the history of the occasion and determined to mark it well, the Boston fans helped launch the first World Series with fervor and enthusiasm. Most prominent among these fans was a group known as the "Royal Rooters," who were cheerfully loud and religiously devoted to their team and who counted among their members a few who were known to have a drink now and then. From within their ranks they raised a band whose musical prowess, by contemporary accounts, was more pleasing to the spirit than to the ear. The Rooters' most popular song was "Tessie," which was sung—relentlessly—to these words:

Tessie, you make me feel so badly,
Why don't you turn around,
Tessie, you know I love you madly,
Babe, my heart weighs about a pound.

Don't blame me if I ever doubt you,
You know I couldn't live without you,
Tessie, you are my only, only, only.

These sterling lyrics were sung constantly during the Series, to the point where some of the Pirate players found themselves being distracted.

"We laughed at first," Pirate third baseman Tommy Leach said, "but after a while it got on our nerves. They kept singing it over and over, and so damned loud. One of the fellows said, 'If I ever meet this gal Tessie, I'm going to punch her in the nose.' "

"I kept hearing those damned words in my sleep all winter," Fred Clarke said.

"I never saw such enthusiastic fans as the ones in Boston," Honus Wagner said.

Even then.

It was a festive occasion at the Huntington Avenue Grounds, which was filled to overflowing. "Brass bands were all over the place," Cy Young said. "Men came in long-tailed

The Huntington Avenue Grounds crowd is all over the field before one of the Series games with Pittsburgh. The crowd around the infield is watching the workout there.
(Courtesy NBL)

Some of the Royal Rooters and their musical accompanists.

coats and high hats or derbies. The ladies were bedecked in their ankle-length skirts and picture hats."

The crowd—it numbered more than 16,000—was so large and the crush at the ticket booths so great that help was needed to keep pace, and among those enlisted were some of the Red Sox players, including Cy Young, who then hurriedly retired to the clubhouse and got into his uniform to start the opening game. (It is true that in many respects baseball has changed little throughout its history; but it is highly unlikely today that the man who sells you your ticket to a World Series game will be the starting pitcher.)

The first World Series began on October 1, 1903. To the dismay and frustration of the locals, the Pirates jumped on Young for four runs in the first inning and then followed the steady pitching of Phillippe to go on to a 7–3 victory.

Dinneen tied the Series the following day with a 3–0 shutout, abetted by two home runs from Patsy Dougherty—which was an example of baseball at its most unpredictable, since

Patsy had hit no homers in 1902 and only four in 1903. In this game, Pittsburgh starter Sam Leever came up with a lame arm, leaving the bulk of the Pirate pitching for the rest of the Series up to Phillippe. (The team's other starter, lefty Ed Doheny, had suffered a mental breakdown late in the season and had been institutionalized.)

John I. Taylor.

Game 3 saw Phillippe put the Pirates back on top with a 4–2 win over Hughes, with Young pitching the last seven innings in relief. Thereafter, every Boston inning for the remainder of the Series would be pitched by either Young or Dinneen.

On October 6 the Series moved to Pittsburgh, where Phillippe gave the Pirates a commanding three-games-to-one lead by pitching his third complete-game victory, beating Dinneen, 5–4.

In Game 5, Young enjoyed an easy 11–2 rout (easy after Boston broke open a scoreless tie with a six-run sixth inning), beating the veteran Bill ("Brickyard") Kennedy, who had been pressed into service as an emergency starter.

The next day Dinneen evened the Series at three games apiece with a 6–3 win over sore-armed Sam Leever. Two days later, still in Pittsburgh, Boston went a game up with a 7–3 win, Young beating Phillippe.

The Series then returned to Boston for Game 8, which proved to be the finale. Dinneen won for the third time, beating the exhausted Phillippe (who pitched a record 44 innings during the Series), 3–0, making Boston the first officially recognized champions of twentieth-century baseball.

As soon as the final out had been recorded, the jubilant Boston fans rushed out onto the field and hoisted their heroes to their shoulders and paraded them around the infield as bands played and the Royal Rooters delivered some more renditions of "Tessie."

Boston's victory over Pittsburgh in that first, long-ago World Series was a landmark achievement in the history of America's favorite game. Not only did it establish once and for all the American League as an equal partner of the National, but the reaction of the public and the press to the concept of a postseason series was overwhelmingly favorable. Pittsburgh manager Fred Clarke might have grumbled (with justification) that it was impossible to win with a one-man pitching staff, but to the public at large the only thing that mattered, as it still does to this day, was who won and who lost.

Pitcher Norwood Gibson (1903–06), who was a 17-game winner in 1904.

There was, however, some tangible balm for the losers. Pittsburgh owner Barney Dreyfuss decided to kick his share of the Series' money into his players' pool, and as a result the Pirate players emerged with individual checks that were greater than those of Boston's—$1,316 to $1,182—the only time the loser's share in a World Series has been larger than the winner's. Henry Killilea pocketed his owner's share, which came to around $6,700.

When word of Dreyfuss's magnanimity got around, it made Killilea look tight-fisted, and Henry soon became unpopular in Boston. But it didn't matter, for he was already in the process of selling the club.

By the opening of the 1904 season the team—still called the Pilgrims—had a new owner, General Charles Henry Taylor, who also owned the *Boston Globe*. Beginning with his service in the Civil War, during which he was wounded, the general had worked himself up into one of Boston's solid citizens. In buying the Pilgrims, he outbid several other prospective buyers, among them John F. ("Honey Fitz") Fitzgerald, later one of Boston's most colorful mayors and grandfather of President John F. Kennedy.

Taylor's purpose in buying the team, in addition to making a very sound business investment, was to provide a diversion for his son, John I. Taylor. Young Taylor was known as a "sportsman," which was a convenient term for one whose lifestyle was not geared toward sainthood. Young Taylor enjoyed golf, tennis, and polo, as well as young ladies, parties, liquid refreshments, and whatever pastimes might emerge from a blend of the latter three. One of his passions was baseball; he was an avid fan of the Pilgrims, and his father hoped that presidency of the club might productively focus the boy's mind.

If it was General Taylor's intention to turn a profit and at the same time keep his son occupied, then in 1904 the old man enjoyed a rousing dual success. The Pilgrims fought a tense, ultimately successful pennant race that so engrossed Boston fans that it drew 623,295 of them to the Huntington Avenue Grounds' ticket windows (the team's second highest attendance until 1936).

Jesse Tannehill (1904–08), Boston's first left-handed ace. (*Courtesy NBL*)

With the American League batting average dropping to .245—it would not get over .250 again until 1911, when a slightly more lively ball was introduced—the Pilgrims followed the arms of their strong pitching staff to a second straight pennant. Cy Young was 26–16; Bill Dinneen, 23–14; and left-handed newcomer Jesse Tannehill, 21–11. Right-handers Norwood Gibson and George Winter were 17–14 and 8–4, respectively. No other pitcher hurled for Boston that year. It was the first year of the 154-game schedule; and with ties included, Boston played 157 games, with its hardy staff completing 148 of them—the all-time major-league record.

Joe Harris (1905–07), who lost 21 games in 1906.

The thirty-seven-year-old Young tossed a league-high 10 shutouts and had a 1.97 ERA, which was bettered by five other starters in that pitcher-dominated year. Along the way, Cy delivered the twentieth century's first perfect game, on May 5, when he laminated the Athletics, 3–0. In the newspaper parlance of the day, Cy "skunked" the A's, with skipper Connie Mack saying, "I have never seen such a game pitched." Nor was he ever to see another like it, though he remained in baseball until 1950.

At one point during the season, Young hurled $45\frac{2}{3}$ consecutive scoreless innings. The old boy was simply superb all season, completing 40 of his 41 starts and walking a parsimonious 29 batters in 380 innings.

On August 17, Tannehill pitched the franchise's second no-hitter as he was defeating the White Sox, 6–0.

The Pilgrims didn't have a .300 hitter, Chick Stahl's .295 being tops. Chick led the league with 22 triples, still the Boston team record (tied by Tris Speaker in 1913).

Chick Stahl (1901–06). Chick was the Red Sox skipper when he died under somewhat curious circumstances in the spring of 1907.

The 1904 pennant race was a cutthroat battle between Boston and New York (then known as the Highlanders), and it went down to the two teams' final confrontation, on the final day of the season (as it would in 1949 and again in 1978). The Pilgrims were at New York's Hilltop Park on October 10 to play a doubleheader. Collins's men held a one-and-a-half-game lead and needed just one win to clinch their second straight pennant. (Boston had played three more games than New York and won them all. In those years, unplayed games that had a bearing on the pennant race were not made up, as they are today.)

Heading the New York staff was right-handed spitballer Jack Chesbro, whose 1904 statistics read like misprints: 41–12 won-lost record, 455 innings pitched, 1.82 ERA, 48 complete games in 51 starts. Even allowing for the fact that in those days pitchers went to the mound more often and stayed out there longer, these numbers are remarkable.

Inevitably, Chesbro started the first game of the doubleheader for New York, with Dinneen going for Boston. As befitted a game that had the weight of the season resting on every pitch, it went into the ninth inning in a 2–2 tie. Lou Criger led off for Boston and singled. He moved around to third on a sacrifice and a ground out.

So there was a man on third and two out, and 41-game winner Jack Chesbro was standing on the mound, working in his 455th inning of the season. Jack lathered up a moist one (the spitter was a legal pitch in those days) and fired. In order for a spitball to be truly effective, it has to be thrown hard, and in this crucial situation Chesbro was obviously giving it all he had. He gave a mite too much, however, for the ball sailed over the head of the catcher, Red Kleinow, allowing Criger to come home with what proved to be the game-winning—the pennant-winning—run.

Along with the rest of the sporting world, the Boston players had been looking forward to another postseason series with the National League champions—in this case, John McGraw's New York Giants. John J., however, was still nursing his grudge against the American League, in general, and against Ban Johnson, in particular, a grudge that had only intensified since the new league had placed another team in New York, a city that McGraw saw as his personal fiefdom.

McGraw had been saying for several weeks that he would not allow his club on the same field with the representatives of what he referred to as "a minor league," "a bush league," and worse. Hardening his stance was the possibility of the American League winners being the Highlanders. He was backed up by Giants' owner John Brush. They were probably the only two men in America not in favor of the Series. The Giant players certainly were: the postseason action would have meant about $1,200 or so per man, about fifty percent of the average salary.

The Boston players called McGraw and Brush "dirty cowards," Ban Johnson accused McGraw of being afraid of suffering the same embarrassment the Pirates had the year before, and the *Sporting News* declared the Boston club "World Champions by default."

The press and the public, who had been avidly looking forward to the Series and in particular to a matchup between Young and McGraw's great right-hander, Christy Mathewson, were bitterly disappointed. The protests were so vociferous that even the dictatorial Mr. McGraw had to take notice. Accordingly, the World Series was renewed the next year (with McGraw's Giants one of the starring teams) and has continued through the decades without interruption.

The Pilgrims had enjoyed solid success during the first four years of their existence, finishing second, then third, then taking two straight pennants. After that, however, came a stretch of lean years before the club realigned itself and went on to the most vibrantly successful years in its history.

The team finished fourth in 1905, with Young falling to an 18–19 record, despite a 1.82 ERA, third best in the league. Cy's problem was the club's problem—feeble hitting—with the team batting just .234, its all-time low mark (equaled by the 1907 edition). Jimmy Collins was high man on the offensive totem pole with a .276 average. Southpaw Jesse Tannehill managed to survive his mates' timid offense and ring up a 22–9 record. Attendance dropped by some 150,000, leading second-year owner John Taylor to state glumly one of baseball's eternal verities: "More people come out to the park when you are winning the pennant."

Things got much worse in 1906: a last-place finish, based on a 49–105 record. The team batted .239, scored the fewest runs in its history (462), hit the fewest home runs (13), were shut out twenty-eight times, and from May 1 through May 24 set an American League record by losing twenty consecutive games (the record was tied by the Philadelphia Athletics of 1916 and 1943). Making those losses even more unpalatable was having the last nineteen of them take place at home.

Symbol of the year's futility for Boston was twenty-four-year-old right-hander Joe Harris, a product of nearby Melrose. The rookie pitcher labored through a nightmare 2–21 season. On September 1, Joe found out once and for all that it wasn't his year. On that day, he dueled Philadelphia's Jack Coombs for twenty-three innings in a 1–1 tie, only to have the A's erupt for three in the top of the twenty-fourth. The game got Joe into the books—he and Coombs hold the American League record for most innings pitched in one game. The affair itself remained on the books as the league's longest by innings until Chicago and Milwaukee went twenty-five in 1984 (played over two days,

Another game has just ended at the Huntington Avenue Grounds. (*Courtesy NBL*)

however). When Harris started the next season going 0–7, the Sox decided to punch his ticket, sending him out of the bigs with a lifetime 3–30 record.

The dismal 1906 season helped sour the relationship between Collins and Taylor. And when the manager and the boss are grumbling at each other and the team is in last place, the inevitable happens. Jimmy resigned late in the season, before he could be canned, and was replaced by Chick Stahl. (Collins was traded to the Athletics the following June.)

The 1907 season started on a note of tragedy: the death in spring training of manager Stahl. The thirty-four-year-old skipper suffered a leg injury, and a doctor gave him a solution of carbolic acid and water as treatment. Obtained from coal tar, carbolic acid was used chiefly as a disinfectant; taken internally, it was poisonous. On March 28, Stahl drank a glass of the solution and an hour later was dead. Whether his death was a tragic accident or suicide will never be known. An accident seems unlikely, yet there was no apparent reason for suicide: Chick Stahl was a deeply religious man, was happily married, and as far as anyone could tell, was relatively untroubled.

It was a chaotic year for the Red Sox, as the team was now officially known. Young filled in as Stahl's replacement at the opening of the season, stipulating it was only temporary until Taylor could find a new skipper. Cy ran things for seven games, and then George Huff, a scout for the Chicago Cubs, was hired. After eight games, Taylor decided Huff was a mistake and fired him. Next, the job was handed to the club's first baseman, Bob Unglaub. Bob managed for twenty-eight games, lost twenty of them, and was told to forget managing and concentrate on first base. He, in turn, was replaced by James ("Deacon") McGuire, forty-one years old and a big leaguer since 1884. This accumulation of brainpower managed to lift the team up a notch, to seventh place.

Fred Lake, Red Sox skipper in 1908 and 1909.

The team was last in batting (.234) and runs (464), but Cy Young was able to transcend this pacifism at home plate and turn in a 22–15 record.

But even as they were declining, the Red Sox were sending a flicker of light into the future. Breaking into seven games in 1907 was a nineteen-year-old outfielder named Tris Speaker, up from the Texas League and soon to become Boston's first truly great all-around player.

The Sox climbed to fifth place in 1908, with McGuire being given the boot in August and Fred Lake replacing him. The Canadian-born Lake, who managed the team through the 1909 season, had been a backup catcher for several National League clubs in the 1890s.

The now forty-one-year-old Cy Young was 21–11 in 1908, his sixteenth and final season of twenty or more victories. Among his wins that year was a no-hitter delivered against New York on June 30, 8–0, a single base on balls depriving him of a second perfect game.

In August, the Red Sox and the rest of the American League players paid a remarkable tribute to Cy. They all chipped in and bought a silver loving cup, which they presented to him in appreciation of his greatness as a pitcher and for the stature he

(Opposite Page) Cy Young, with the silver loving cup presented to him in 1908 by his teammates and the other American League players, in tribute to his stature and achievements.

BOSTON

Nineteen-year-old Joe Wood (1908–15) in 1909.

had brought to baseball. It was a touching gesture, especially coming from men whose professional reputation at the time painted them as coarse and socially undesirable. (Very few first-rate hotels would accept them as guests.)

The esteem of his peers notwithstanding, Cy found himself sold to Cleveland after the season for $12,500. During his eight years with Boston, Cy logged a 193–112 sheet, and since then no pitcher has won more games, or lost more, in a Red Sox uniform.

(OPPOSITE PAGE) Fifteen-year-old George Herman Ruth on the ball field at St. Mary's Industrial School in Baltimore. The year was 1910.

Even as Young was departing, Joe Wood was arriving. In 1908, the handsome eighteen-year-old right-hander with the

fastball that would soon earn him the nickname "Smoky" was purchased by the Red Sox from Kansas City in the American Association. Young Joe showed up at the end of the season and was 1–1—the victory, significantly, a shutout.

They were ships passing in a brief night, Cy Young and Joe Wood, teammates for several weeks.

"No, he didn't pay much attention to me," Wood said in an interview years later. "I don't think we talked to one another at all. I was just an unknown kid coming onto the club." That's the way it was in those days, Wood said—a rookie had all the stature of a dented water bucket. But a few years later, all of baseball, Cy Young included, would pay attention to Joe Wood.

The Sox climbed to third place in 1909, after which Lake left to manage Boston's National League entry. By the end of the season, not one player from the 1903–04 pennant winners was with the Red Sox. Averaging twenty-six years of age, the Red Sox were the youngest team in the league, and among these young ballplayers were several who would lead the club into the most successful decade in its history. Playing his first full season, center fielder Tris Speaker batted .309, while Joe Wood broke in with an 11–7 record. Playing half the season was twenty-one-year-old right fielder Harry Hooper, twenty-five-year-old Bill Carrigan was catching, and twenty-three-year-old Larry Gardner got into a few games at third base.

And while this nucleus was forming, the man who would soon become the team's ace left-hander and who would go on to rock the foundations of baseball was biding his time as a fifteen-year-old resident of St. Mary's Industrial School, a home for wayward boys in Baltimore. As the school's ace pitcher and star slugger, George Herman Ruth was getting ready.

— 3 —

Years of Glory

The Red Sox' great decade began quietly, with a fourth-place finish in 1910 under new manager Patsy Donovan. The ace of the staff that year was right-hander Eddie Cicotte (15–11). The Red Sox were to become so rich in pitching that two years later they were able to sell Eddie to the White Sox, where he became one of the league's top winners before falling into the abyss of the scandalous 1919 World Series. Joe Wood was only 12–13 but was already regarded as one of the league's hardest throwers.

First baseman Jake Stahl (brother of the late Chick) hit 10 home runs to lead the league, giving the club its second home-run champion (there have been seventeen). Larry Gardner played his first full season for Boston, as a second baseman. In 1911, he switched to third, which remained his position until he retired in 1924. Larry was exceptionally quick around the bag, with an uncanny knack for swooping in on bunts dropped down by Ty Cobb and nipping the great man at first base. Years later, after both he and Cobb had retired, Larry explained his success: "When Ty was going to bunt, he'd always lock his lips. When I saw that, I'd start in with the pitch. He never realized I'd caught on."

Harry Hooper played his first full season and set a standard for covering right field that wasn't equaled in Boston until the arrival of Dwight Evans more than sixty years later. Taking over in left field was Duffy Lewis, who soon built a reputation as one of the game's toughest clutch hitters. (What makes an otherwise average player consistently excel in critical situations remains unexplained, in baseball or any other sport. Perhaps pressure and pride are alchemized in some athletes in a reaction as yet undiscovered by science. Whatever the explanation, Duffy Lewis was the man his teammates wanted to see at the plate when the gold ring was up for grabs.)

When it came to playing left field, it was said that Lewis had no master. He and Hooper and Speaker soon became celebrated for their defensive magic, and in baseball there is no defensive

(OPPOSITE PAGE) Eddie Cicotte (1908–12), who pitched well for Boston, then went on to greatness and infamy with the White Sox.

magic more thrilling than that of the outfield, with its opportunities for pursuit and its leaps and dives and tumbles. Speaker, a .340 hitter in 1910, was now the star of the team and soon to be, next to Cobb, the league's premier player. With a .344 lifetime batting average for his twenty-two-year career, "Spoke" was for a long time the automatic choice as center fielder in baseball's all-time outfield (flanked by Ruth and Cobb), though some latter-day selectors would replace him with either Joe DiMaggio or Willie Mays.

Patsy Donovan, Red Sox manager in 1910 and 1911.

Speaker was blessed with great speed afoot and used it to play an extremely shallow center field, even by the standards of the dead-ball era. (Teammates swore they never saw a ball hit over his head.) He played in so far that he was able on several occasions to turn in unassisted double plays. He also possessed a powerful throwing arm—his 448 lifetime assists stand as the major-league record, and his 35 assists in 1912 have never been bettered in the American League. In addition, his 793 career doubles are far and away the major-league record.

Harry Hooper (1909–20).

The Sox finished fifth in 1911, with Joe Wood hanging up a 23–17 record, including a no-hitter over the St. Louis Browns on July 29. In another game, Joe chalked up 15 strikeouts, which remained the club record until Bill Monbouquette broke it with 17 in 1961. The young fireballer was now on the brink of a greatness that would be all too fleeting—so fleeting, in fact, that it made him a mythic figure in Boston baseball, a man frozen by injury into a sort of eternal youth.

The team lost the services of its first baseman, as Jake Stahl retired for one year to work in a Chicago bank run by his in-laws. He returned, however, in 1912 and took over as manager, the job held briefly by his late brother, Chick; the only instance in big-league history of two brothers having managed the same team.

The big news of 1911 was the announcement that the Red Sox were to have a new home. Just before he sold the club to former big-league ballplayer and manager Jimmy McAleer,

(OPPOSITE PAGE) Tris Speaker (1907–15). *(Courtesy NBL)*

RED SO

John Taylor decided the team needed a more seemly home field and authorized the construction of a new one.

The site of what was eventually to become one of baseball's most storied ballparks and, with the passage of time, the most charming, was the corner of Landsdowne and Jersey streets, in the city's Fenway section. It was Taylor who decided it should be called Fenway Park.

Smoky Joe Wood (1908–15). A brief, unforgettable career.

Fenway's most famous feature, its neighborly left-field wall (the "Green Monster"), was there from the beginning, although its 320-foot distance and thirty-seven-foot height made it a much more formidable target in the dead-ball era than it would be later on. (A twenty-three-foot-tall screen was draped above the wall in 1936 to help reduce window breakage on Landsdowne Street.)

Jimmy McAleer.

The proximity of Fenway's left-field wall has helped shape Red Sox history, as through the years the team has placed a heavy emphasis on right-handed hitting. Among those hitters were many who became overly distracted by the beckoning wall and went to early professional graves by trying to pull low, outside breaking pitches. By tailoring their lineup to their Fenway haven, the Red Sox have through the years proved to be exceptionally tough to beat at home. But this blueprint for success at home has cost them on the road, where their won-lost record has never been as good.

Fenway Park underwent major reconstruction in time for the opening of the 1934 season. The park's new look included enlargement of the grandstand from the left-field wall around to right field, with the wooden center-field stands being replaced by concrete bleachers. Other work included the leveling of a ten-foot embankment that ran to the base of the left-field wall, a quite perceptible rise that had been bedeviling left fielders since 1912 and was known as "Duffy's Cliff," for Duffy Lewis, who had played it so well. (Playing it well included not tumbling on your keister, as some visiting left fielders had been known to do.)

"Left field giveth and right field taketh away" might well have been the motto of Fenway, for the right-field power alley was of disheartening distance. While it was only 302 feet down the line, the breakaway was sudden and sharp, slicing out to around 390 feet in right-center. In deference to the booming bat of young Ted Williams, this distance was reduced by approximately ten feet in 1940, and fenced-in bullpens—"Williamsburg"—were built in front of the bleachers in right and right-center.

Hugh Bradley (1910–12), who hit the first home run ever struck in Fenway Park. Hitting one over the wall in the dead ball era was considered something of a feat.

But let's return to April 20, 1912, when, after a couple of rain delays, the new home of the Boston Red Sox officially opened for business, with the locals beating the Yankees, 7–6, in eleven innings. (Unfortunately, the grand occasion had to share newspaper space with reports of the sinking of the *Titanic.*)

Fenway Park's first home run was recorded on April 26, by light-hitting back-up first baseman Hugh Bradley. It was Bradley's only home run of the season, but it earned him a place in Red Sox annals.

The Red Sox inaugurated their new home in spectacular fashion, winning a team-record 105 games and sprinting to an easy pennant, finishing fourteen games ahead of second-place Washington, for whom Walter Johnson was 32–12. Walter, however, was not the league's top pitcher that year, as Smoky Joe Wood fired his way to a searing 34–5 record, one of the greatest seasons ever enjoyed by a big-league pitcher. It was the year that emblazoned the name Joe Wood forever on the tapestries of Red Sox history. (More than seventy years later, in 1984, a sell-out Fenway crowd would rise to its feet on Old-Timers Day to cheer the ninety-four-year-old Joe Wood as he was driven around the field he had once so brilliantly dominated.)

Speaker was the team's cutting edge, batting .383 and tying for the league home-run lead with 10. Gardner batted .315 and manager–first baseman Stahl, .301. Steve Yerkes was at second, Heinie Wagner at short, and tough Bill Carrigan behind the plate, with Hooper and Lewis joining with Speaker to form

Boston's 1912 pitching staff lines up to oblige the photographer. (*Left to right*) Larry Pape, Hugh Bedient, Buck O'Brien, Charley Hall, Ray Collins, Joe Wood. (*Courtesy NBL*)

what many a white-haired old-timer went to the grave swearing was the greatest defensive outfield ever.

Boston's pride that year was its pitching, for behind Wood were Hugh Bedient (20–9), Buck O'Brien (20–13), Charley Hall (15–8), and left-hander Ray Collins (13–8).

The team got off to a good start in April (9–4) and May (16–9) and then really poured on the coal, going 21–8 in June, 21–9 in July, and 20–7 in August, by which time the race was over. Much of that consistent winning was attributable to Wood, who, once he began winning, became simply unbeatable. By early September he had won thirteen straight and was heading directly for the American League record of sixteen straight, which had been set by Walter Johnson just a few days earlier. (Walter's win skein had come to an end on August 23.)

Heinie Wagner (1906–13, 1915–16, 1918), shortstop on the 1912 pennant winner. Heinie also managed the Sox in 1930.

On September 6, baseball's two premier fireballers met head-on in one of the most dramatic pitching duels in history. Wood was going for his fourteenth consecutive victory; the opposition was the Washington Senators, with Johnson on the mound.

"It was on a Friday," Wood recalled years later. "My regular pitching turn was scheduled to come on Saturday, but they moved it up a day so that Walter and I could face each other. Walter had already won sixteen in a row, and his streak had ended. I had won thirteen in a row, and they challenged our manager to pitch me against Walter.

"The newspapers publicized us like prizefighters: giving statistics comparing our height, weight, biceps, triceps, arm span and whatnot. The Champion, Walter Johnson, versus the Challenger, Joe Wood."

Duffy Lewis (1910–17). Duffy's best year was 1911, when he hit .307.

Needless to say, an overflow crowd packed Fenway that long-ago afternoon to watch baseball's fastest guns measure off at sixty feet. It was, as one writer was to put it years later, "Louis and Dempsey in spiked shoes."

Ropes were strung across the outfield to create standing room to accommodate some of the estimated 30,000 fans who had paid their way in to see what was sure to be a historic pitching confrontation. Hundreds of fans were allowed onto the

Duffy Lewis (*left*) relaxing with catchers Chester (Pinch) Thomas (1912–17) and Forrest ("Hick") Cady (1912–17). (*Courtesy NBL*)

field, jamming the foul-line areas in front of the grandstand between first base and third base, forcing the teams to abandon their dugouts and sit on benches alongside the lines.

The star performers rose to the occasion, treating the enthralled gathering to what was dramatically correct—a 1–0 game, won by Wood and the Red Sox on two-out, back-to-back doubles by Speaker and Lewis in the sixth inning.

Smoky Joe Wood.

After notching this memorable fourteenth-straight victory, Wood went on to tie Johnson's record with two more wins before being stopped by Detroit on September 20 by a 6–4 score. Sixteen consecutive victories still stands as the American League record for pitchers, tied by Philadelphia's Lefty Grove in 1931 and Detroit's Schoolboy Rowe in 1934. (Interestingly, the major-league record of nineteen straight wins was set in that same 1912 season, by the New York Giants' Rube Marquard.)

The 1912 postseason contest between the Boston Red Sox and New York Giants stands as the first "greatest World Series of all time." John McGraw's Giants were in the midst of a string of three straight pennants, with the club featuring on the mound, in addition to the 26-game-winning Marquard and superb rookie spitballer Jeff Tesreau (17–7), the illustrious Christy Mathewson. Now thirty-two years old, Mathewson was showing signs of slowing down, which in his case meant a 23–12 record, his second lowest win total in ten years.

McGraw's was an aggressive club that included catcher John ("Chief") Meyers, whose .358 batting average remains the highest ever for a National League catcher; first baseman Fred Merkle; second baseman Larry Doyle; shortstop Art Fletcher; third baseman Buck Herzog; and outfielders Josh Devore, Red Murray, and Fred Snodgrass. These Giants were rabbits on the basepaths, stealing 319 bases.

Young Joe Wood, his own 34 wins safely in the bank, was awed by the great Mathewson. "I don't think he was as fast as he once had been," Joe said. "When I saw him his greatest asset was control and a beautiful curve ball that he'd start over your

(Opposite page) Joe Wood (*left*) and Walter Johnson meeting before their memorable September 6, 1912, duel at Fenway.

W

head and bring right down. I'd never seen a curve ball like it. He also threw what they called a fadeaway, which is the same as a screwball. As far as I know, he was the only one who threw it at that time."

(OPPOSITE PAGE) Joe Wood warming up amid the overflow crowd for his famous match with Walter Johnson.

McGraw pulled a surprise by opening the Series with Tesreau, while Stahl led with his ace, Joe Wood. Smoky Joe got Boston off to a winning start with a 4–3 win in New York's Polo Grounds, fanning the game's last two batters in the bottom of the ninth with the tying and winning runs on second and third. "I was just burning them in and hoping for the best," Wood said. He was throwing so hard, "I thought my arm would fly right off my body."

The next day, in Boston, the clubs played to a 6–6, eleven-inning tie, called because of darkness. Then Marquard tied the Series with a 2–1 win over Buck O'Brien. Wood came back and put the Sox one up with a 3–1 win over Tesreau. Boston then took a commanding three-games-to-one lead when Bedient nipped Mathewson, 2–1.

The Giants came fighting back to tie the Series at three games apiece as Marquard beat O'Brien, 5–2, and Tesreau beat Wood, 11–4. The latter game, played in Boston, saw some noisy, angry controversy before a pitch was thrown.

"It seems," Joe Wood said, "that more tickets had been sold than there were seats, and it so happened that the people who were shut out were the Royal Rooters. Well, it took the mounted police to get them to go and when they finally did go they took part of the center field fence with them. I was all warmed up and ready to start pitching, and then that crowd broke down the fence. I had to go and sit down on the bench until it was fixed. Some people said that was why I got hit so hard in the first inning"—Joe was nailed for six runs in the top of the first—"that I had cooled off. But I don't think that had anything to do with it."

Bill Carrigan (1906, 1908–16). They called him "Rough."

So the scene was now primed for the deciding game, to be played at Fenway Park. McGraw sent Mathewson to the mound, while Stahl started Bedient.

The Giants opened up a 1–0 lead in the top of the third, and Mathewson nursed it along until the bottom of the seventh. Boston got two men on and Stahl sent reserve outfielder Olaf Henriksen up to hit for Bedient. In his one and only time at bat in the Series, Henriksen delivered a shot down the left-field line for a game-tying double. Mathewson then retired the side.

With the world championship now balanced on single pitches, Stahl sent Wood to the mound for the fourth time in the Series. Young Wood and the veteran Mathewson dueled on even terms through the eighth and ninth innings. In the top of the tenth, the Giants scored on a double by Murray and a single by Merkle. Wood then knocked down a hard shot to the mound and made the third out, but in doing so hurt his hand, a play that was to become pivotal a few minutes later.

Needing one run to stay alive, the Sox came to bat in the last of the tenth, facing a supremely confident Mathewson. Wood was scheduled to lead off and normally would have batted for himself—the ace pitcher was a superb all-around athlete and a .290 batter that season. But because of his injured hand, Joe could not bat. In his place, Stahl sent up Clyde Engle, a little-used utility infielder. Engle lifted an easy fly ball to center field where the usually sure-handed Fred Snodgrass drifted under it. To everyone's amazement, the ball struck Snodgrass's glove and dropped to the ground. Engle made it to second base.

Hooper was next up for Boston, and Harry lined one that looked as though it was going to carry over Snodgrass's head in center. But now, in a complete reversal of form, the New York center fielder raced back and made a sensational over-the-shoulder catch on the dead run. (Decades later, fellow Californians Snodgrass and Hooper ran into each other, and Snodgrass smiled wryly and said, "Nobody remembers the one I caught, do they?" According to Hooper, "He had no business catching that ball. But in some way, I don't know how, he did." But Snodgrass was right, for subsequent events soon rendered his great play irrelevant, and today it is almost totally forgotten.)

Hugh Bedient (1912–14), who was a 20-game winner in his rookie year.

The career of Buck O'Brien, a 20-game winner in 1912, lasted just three years (1911–13).

Right-hander Charley Hall (1909–13), whose 15–8 record in 1912 was the best of his career.

Rival managers Jake Stahl (*left*) and John McGraw doing the traditional thing before the start of the 1912 World Series. (*Courtesy NBL*)

Joe Wood (*left*) and Christy Mathewson at the 1912 World Series.

After Hooper's drive had been caught, Engle tagged up and went to third. Steve Yerkes, the potential winning run, drew a walk. Now came another critical mistake by the Giants. With the tying run on third and one out, Speaker lifted a little pop foul between first and home. Joe Wood, sitting on the bench clutching his throbbing hand, never forgot what happened.

"The first baseman, Fred Merkle, had the best shot at it. But instead of calling for Merkle to take it, Mathewson came down off the mound calling for Chief Meyers, the catcher. Merkle could have caught it easily, but Mathewson kept calling for Meyers, I'll never know why. You see, Merkle was coming in on the ball and the Chief was going with it. It's a much easier play for Merkle. But there was Matty, yelling for the Chief. I can hear him to this day. But Meyers never could get to it. The ball dropped. It just clunked down into the grass in foul ground and lay there. We couldn't believe it. Neither could Mathewson. You never saw a man as mad as he was when that ball hit the ground. But the way we saw it, it was his own fault. He called for the wrong man."

Meyers walked disconsolately back to his position behind the plate. The fine old catcher later remembered: "I kind of squinched up one eye and looked at Speaker standing there and thought to myself, 'You don't give this fellow two swings for the price of one.' "

Boston's utility outfielder, Olaf Henriksen (1911–17). He was born in Denmark, but his nickname was "Swede."

The Chief was right—Speaker lined a single to right to tie the game. On the throw to third trying to get Yerkes, Speaker went to second. McGraw then ordered Duffy Lewis walked to fill the bases, hoping for a double-play ball. But Larry Gardner would not oblige. "Always a dependable fellow," according to a teammate, Gardner lifted a fly to deep right that scored Yerkes with the winning run.

And so ended what was, according to *Reach's 1913 Official American League Guide,* "the most desperately contested World Series on record."

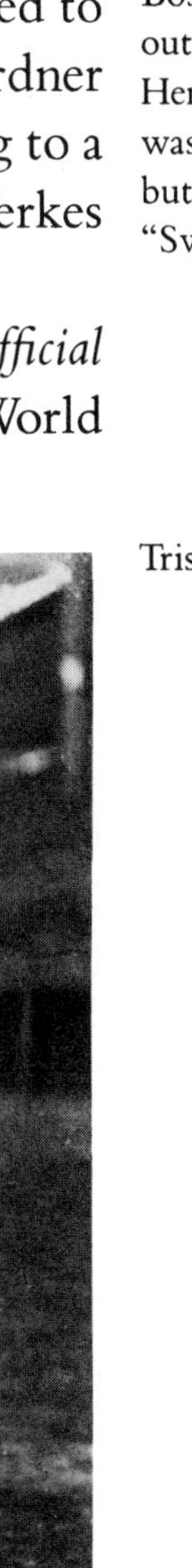

Tris Speaker.

That wondrous 1912 season proved to be only an interlude in the ongoing domination of the American League by the Philadelphia Athletics. Connie Mack's team, which had won pennants in 1910 and 1911, finished third to Boston's 1912 runaway, then came back to win again in 1913 and 1914.

Boston's hopes for repeating in 1913 were doomed in spring training, when Joe Wood, trying to field a bunt, slipped on wet grass and broke his thumb. From that moment on, Wood was no longer the pitcher he had been in 1912. Some people felt the club rushed him back too quickly after the injury, for he soon developed a sore shoulder. He could still throw hard, but at the cost of pain so severe his arm sometimes needed several weeks to recuperate. When he was able to pitch, he was effective, as his records for the next three years indicate: 11–5, 9–3, 15–5. But the club finally decided it could not afford to carry (or pay) a pitcher who averaged only sixteen starts a year, and when it tried to cut his salary in 1916, Wood held out for the entire year. In February 1917, he was sold for $15,000 to Cleveland, where he became a part-time outfielder. But for one bright and unforgettable year, Joe Wood had been the equal of Walter Johnson. Not until the arrival of Roger Clemens almost three-quarters of a century later would the Red Sox again have so dominant a pitcher.

Without Wood, the staff leader in 1913 was lefty Ray Collins (19–8), followed by Bedient (15–14) and newcomer Hubert ("Dutch") Leonard, a left-hander who was 14–16. The club finished a disappointing fourth, with Speaker doing most of the hitting (.365).

During the summer of 1913, McAleer began hearing rumors that Stahl was interested in buying the club. The owner and the manager had been bickering most of the season, and now McAleer, perturbed by the rumors, suddenly canned his skipper and replaced him with Bill Carrigan.

A 1907 graduate of Holy Cross, Carrigan was a Maine-born Irishman with a natural flair for leadership. Quiet and gentlemanly though he was, his pugnacious lantern jaw, coolly

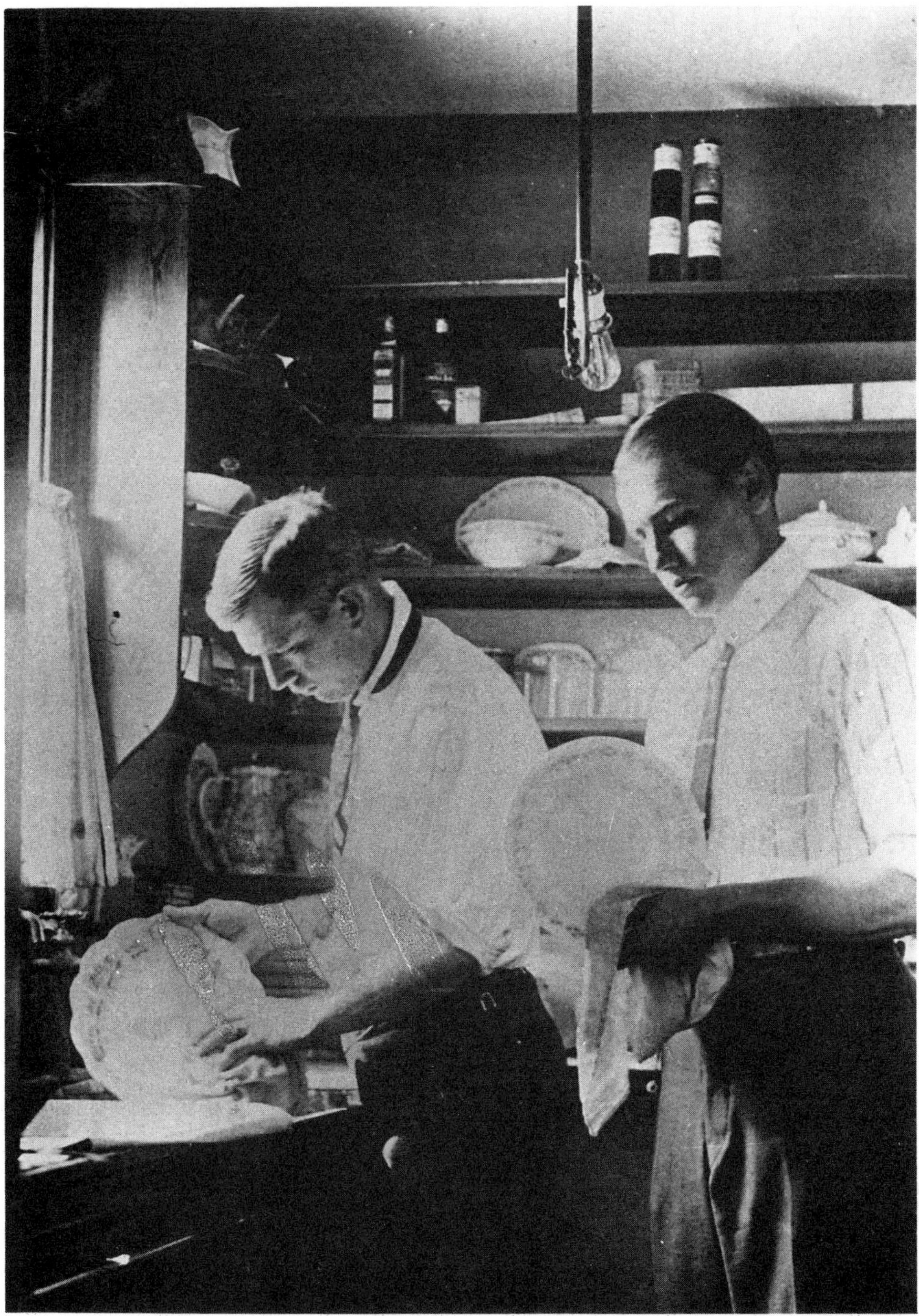

Tris Speaker (*left*) and Joe Wood were best friends and roommates.

observant eyes, and businesslike demeanor proclaimed him a man not to be trifled with. His fair-minded, no-nonsense approach to the game and his own tough, uncompromising style of play quickly earned him the respect of his men. "He was tops," pitcher Ernie Shore, who joined the club in 1914, said of the man known as "Rough." "Best manager in the world."

The club Carrigan inherited had its greatest strength in the outfield—the Speaker-Hooper-Lewis trio, who that year combined for 84 assists, a major-league record that still stands.

Unlike most managers, Carrigan survived a change in ownership, as the Red Sox were sold after the 1913 season to a Quebec-born businessman named Joseph J. Lannin. Lannin, who paid approximately $200,000 for the team, had made a pile in real estate in New York City and on Long Island. In Boston, he found himself walking into a large-size headache.

In a throwback to the freewheeling days when leagues appeared and disappeared, a brand-new outfit called the Federal League made its debut in 1914, proclaiming itself a major league. Naturally, there was outrage and indignation from the established majors (Ban Johnson, who probably overlooked the delicacy of the irony, was one of the more fervent fist-shakers), since the new league had well-padded pockets and a willingness to spend.

However, the Feds, who made the last serious challenge to the big-league structure, were doomed to failure, pulling down the shades after just two years. Although they lured into their fold a number of big leaguers, they were unable to attract the first-magnitude stars such as Cobb, Johnson, Speaker, Eddie Collins, and Honus Wagner, and without these top marquee names there was little hope of drawing crowds.

Despite its quick demise, and despite the fact that it made no serious inroads into the Red Sox roster, the Federal League did create certain shock waves that would eventually be felt in Fenway Park.

With the Federal League, and its seductive checkbooks, competing for players, salaries naturally went up. Speaker, who was earning about $9,000, was courted by the Feds and was able to use this as leverage to get more money out of Lannin, who did not want to lose his star center fielder. Tris demanded and got a two-year contract for 1914–15 that called for $36,000. Thereafter, Lannin curled his lip every time he looked at Tris.

When the Federal League went the way of the dodo bird after the 1915 season, Lannin reassumed the hammer and reduced Speaker's salary to $9,000. A squabble ensued, and at the start of the 1916 season Tris was abruptly dealt to Cleveland.

In 1914, another fallout from the short-lived Federal League hit Boston, this time a beneficial one. The Feds had established a team in Baltimore, where it was in competition with the Baltimore Orioles of the International League, an independently owned club run by Jack Dunn. With a self-proclaimed major-league competitor in town, Oriole attendance fell off sharply. Feeling a cash pinch, Dunn was forced to put several of his younger players on the market before he was ready to. So for $8,000 he sold to the Red Sox catcher Ben Egan, right-hander Ernie Shore, and nineteen-year-old left-hander George Herman "Babe" Ruth.

Young Ruth was in his first year of pro ball. The rollicking, uninhibited youngster had been discovered by Dunn pitching for the St. Mary's team. Located in Baltimore, St. Mary's was an industrial school and home for troublesome youngsters. By the time he was eight years old, George had proved himself too unruly for parental handling and was enrolled in the school, which was run by the Xaverian Brothers, a Catholic order. (Actually, St. Mary's was nonsectarian, open to boys of all denominations. An earlier resident had been a youngster named Asa Yolson, later known to the world as Al Jolson.)

Along with a full curriculum of classroom work and industrial training, St. Mary's had a wide-ranging athletic program. A natural athlete, Ruth participated in football, basketball, and baseball. The boy gradually displayed total mastery of the latter game, becoming the school's star pitcher as well as a slugging, agile outfielder.

It was the pitcher that enchanted Dunn, and the Baltimore Orioles' owner went to St. Mary's, spoke to the Xaverians (who were by this time young Ruth's legal guardians), and asked if they would permit Ruth to sign a contract with the

RED SO

Orioles. Knowing Dunn to be a responsible and honorable man, the Brothers consented. Dunn promised to look after the youngster, and he kept his word, to the extent that Ruth soon became known among the Oriole players as "Dunn's baby" (hence the origin of the famous nickname).

(OPPOSITE PAGE) Rookie Babe Ruth in 1914. He was with the Red Sox until 1919.

Ruth was an instant success on the Baltimore mound, winning 14 games by early July, at which time Dunn made his deal with Boston.

Even as a rookie, Ruth, destined to become the most storied athlete in history, made an indelible impression.

"He had never been anywhere," Harry Hooper said, "didn't know anything about manners or how to behave among people—just a big overgrown green pea. You probably remember him with that big belly he got later on. But that wasn't there in 1914. George was 6′ 2″ and weighed 198 pounds, all of it muscle. He had a slim waist, huge biceps, and no self-discipline, and not much education—not so very different from a lot of other nineteen-year-old would-be ballplayers. Except for two things: he could eat more than anyone else, and he could hit a baseball further."

Larry Gardner had this memory of the young rookie pitcher: "When he hit one, you could hear it all over the park. That's really the first thing I can remember about him—the sound when he'd get a hold of one. It was just different, that's all."

But for the moment, Ruth was there not for his appetite or his bat but for his pitching. The young man, according to Ernie Shore, "could fire the ball as hard as anyone. If he hadn't got to the Hall of Fame with his bat, he would have made it by his pitching, you can be sure of that."

Ruth stayed with Boston for just a few weeks in 1914, then was sent down to Providence of the International League. He was recalled at the end of the season. Overall, he worked 23 innings for the Red Sox, posting a 2–1 record and a 3.91 ERA.

Carrigan lifted the club to second place in 1914, thanks primarily to a strong pitching staff, which had a collective ERA of 2.35, lowest in the league. Lefty Ray Collins was the big winner (20–13, including two complete-game victories over Detroit on September 22 by scores of 5–3 and 5–0), but the star of the staff was Dutch Leonard, who posted a 19–5 record and the lowest earned run average in big-league history—1.01 for 223 innings of work. Right-handers Rube Foster and Ernie Shore were 14–8 and 10–4, respectively. Hugh Bedient was 8–12 and then jumped to the Federal League. The Red Sox were so steeped in mound talent for the next few years that the loss of Collins to injury the following year, the departure of Bedient, and diminishing returns from Wood made little difference.

Left-hander Ray Collins (1909–15), who was a 20-game winner in 1914. (*Courtesy NBL*)

There were a few new faces in the lineup, including first baseman Dick Hoblitzell, obtained from Cincinnati in a mid-season waiver deal, and shortstop Everett Scott. First in the line of outstanding Red Sox shortstops, the twenty-one-year-old Scott was an excellent fielder and a most durable performer—he played in 1,307 consecutive games, which was the endurance record that was finally broken by Lou Gehrig (who went on to play in 2,130 straight games).

There were further vibrations from the tottering Federal League in 1915, and once again they redounded to the benefit of the Red Sox. After taking four pennants in five years (interrupted only by the 1912 Red Sox), Connie Mack began breaking up his powerful Athletics team. There were several reasons behind Connie's dismantling of the Athletics, one of them being the salary war with the Federals, a war the always tight-fisted A's skipper (and part-owner) chose not to engage in.

That's the skipper, Bill Carrigan, giving the troops a pregame workout. In those days, a team seldom carried more than one coach and managers had to work harder.

Among the notables of Mack's 1914 pennant winner who played elsewhere in 1915 were second baseman Eddie Collins (sold to the White Sox), ace pitchers Eddie Plank and Chief Bender (Connie allowed the Feds to outbid him for them), and the gifted shortstop Jack Barry, whom Lannin acquired for Boston for $8,000 in a July 2, 1915, deal, and who was converted to a second baseman by Carrigan.

With the Athletics no longer a factor in the 1915 pennant race, the Red Sox and Tigers settled in for a long, bruising battle for the top spot. Carrigan's team took over first place at the end of July and thanks to a 41–13 August and September were able to hold off Ty Cobb and the rest of the Tigers, finishing with a 101–50 record to Detroit's 100–54, making the Tigers the first team to win 100 games and finish second, which for them was more distinction than consolation.

First baseman Dick Hoblitzell (1914–18).

The Tigers outhit the Sox, .268 to .260, but Boston was stronger where it all boils down to—on the mound. Carrigan's staff was led by Foster and Shore, each of whom was 19–8, followed by young Ruth at 18–8, Leonard at 15–7, and sore-armed Joe Wood, who was 15–5, with a league-leading 1.49 ERA. In addition, Boston added to the staff that year a couple of young pitchers with long, productive careers ahead of them: right-hander Carl Mays and lefty Herb Pennock.

Shortstop Everett Scott (1914–21).

Speaker's .322 average led the club, and when Ruth was on the mound the Sox had another strong bat in the lineup. In 92 at-bats, Babe hit for a .315 average and had four home runs, which was only three fewer than the league leader, one Braggo Roth. The Red Sox as a team hit only fourteen one-way shots; that four of them were struck by a pitcher was highly noticeable.

"I'd say that by 1915 he was already the most popular player on the team," Shore said of Ruth. "More than Speaker or Hooper or Lewis or any of them. We'd come out on the field to warm up and you could hear them all over the park: 'Babe, hey, Babe.' And he'd always turn around and wave and give them that big smile. They loved him and he loved them. That was the secret of the Babe Ruth magic—genuine feeling on both sides. It wasn't ego with the Babe; never say that. It was just the sheer joy of being on a ball field and relating to people. That was his gift, as much as hitting home runs."

Larry Gardner (1908–17)—"Always a dependable fellow" (in the words of one teammate). Larry's best mark for Boston was .315 in 1912. *(Courtesy NBL)*

Ruth's only appearance in the 1915 World Series against the Philadelphia Phillies, however, was as a pinch hitter in the ninth

That's Jack Barry being tagged out at home by Detroit's Oscar Stanage.

inning of the opener. (He grounded out.) With so much quality pitching at his disposal, Carrigan was able to win it without using his left-handed ace, despite Ruth's pleas for a start.

Shore pitched the opener against the Phillies' great right-hander Grover Cleveland Alexander (a 31-game winner that year) and lost, 3–1, when Philadelphia scored two runs in the bottom of the eighth on a series of infield bleeders.

The next day Foster pitched a three-hitter for the Sox and won, 2–1, driving in the winning run with his own single in the top of the ninth. This game saw a bit of history when Woodrow Wilson became the first president ever to attend a World Series game. The start of the game was delayed for twenty minutes by Wilson's tardy arrival, something no president would dare do today. (Nor would a World Series game be delayed for any mere mortal. American priorities have changed.)

Tris Speaker.
(*Courtesy NBL*)

Harry Hooper.
(*Courtesy NBL*)

The teams then boarded the train for Boston, though not for Fenway Park. The Boston Braves had in August opened their new park, Braves Field, and because its seating capacity was much larger than Fenway's, it was chosen as the site of games 3 and 4.

"Some of our fans grumbled about not having the games at Fenway," Shore said, "but the players were happy about it because more tickets would be sold and we shared in the receipts. After all, baseball was a business." Even in 1915.

Utility infielder Hal Janvrin (1911, 1913–17). He was the first player to go directly from high school to the big leagues. (*Courtesy NBL*)

Game 3 drew 42,300 fans to Braves Field—a new World Series attendance record—and they saw Leonard retire the last twenty batters he faced and whip Alexander, 2–1, the winning run scoring on Lewis's single in the bottom of the ninth.

Game 4 earned the Series the title "The 2–1 Series," when Boston won by that score for the third straight time. Shore pitched a strong game, with the deciding run coming in on Lewis's double in the bottom of the sixth. It was this kind of "bingling" that earned Duffy his reputation as Boston's meat-and-potatoes hitter.

Boston wrapped it up in Philadelphia the next day, coming from behind in the late innings to give Foster a 5–4 win. For a club that had hit just fourteen home runs all season, the Sox won this one in uncharacteristic fashion—on home runs, two by Hooper and one by Lewis. Harry's pair of solo shots went into the temporary bleachers the Phillies had erected in center field, his second one breaking a 4–4 tie in the top of the ninth. Lewis, the hitting star of the Series, had tied it with a two-run blast in the top of the eighth.

Ruth, who seldom evaluated the talent around him, said in later years that the 1915 Red Sox were "the greatest defensive team of all time." Ty Cobb agreed with him, citing in particular Larry Gardner and Everett Scott on the left side of the infield, and the prowess of the Speaker-Hooper-Lewis outfield.

George ("Rube") Foster (1913–17), an ace pitcher on Boston's 1915 and 1916 pennant winners.

With the Federal League being laid to rest unmourned and in an unmarked grave after the 1915 season, the salary wars

Dutch Leonard (1913–18), who in 1914 posted baseball's all-time lowest ERA (1.01).

Manager Carrigan (*right*) receiving an award. Standing behind the young boy is Babe Ruth, and to the Babe's left are Hick Cady, Ernie Shore, and club owner Joseph Lannin.

came to an end. The established majors once again held the upper hand, and in that hand was an instrument for cutting salaries. One of the most prominent differences of contractual opinion was the one between Tris Speaker and Red Sox owner Joseph Lannin. Just when it seemed that the club had come to an accommodation with its star center fielder, Lannin stunned Red Sox fans with the announcement on April 12, 1916, that Speaker had been shipped to Cleveland for infielder Fred Thomas, right-handed pitcher Sam Jones, and $55,000, which was a truckload of money in those days.

Red Sox fans were shocked, infuriated, and depressed by the loss of their star player (and in all of baseball, only Cobb was better). Among other things, Speaker's departure broke up the pride and joy of Boston baseball—the impermeable outfield of Speaker, Lewis, and Hooper, that swift and sure alignment that never seemed to turn its backs on the infield except when making a breathtaking catch on some hellbent fly ball.

Replacing Speaker in center field was Clarence ("Tilly") Walker, whom the Sox obtained from the St. Louis Browns. Tilly was an able man, but no Speaker, who went on to bat .386 for Cleveland and lead the league in batting, the only man other than Cobb to win an American League batting championship between 1907 and 1919.

Despite the loss of Speaker, the Red Sox survived a grueling three-way fight with Chicago and Detroit and won their second straight pennant, finishing two games ahead of the White Sox and four ahead of the Tigers.

Duffy Lewis. (*Courtesy NBL*)

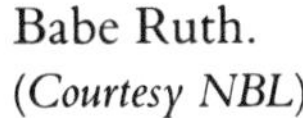

Babe Ruth. (*Courtesy NBL*)

(Opposite page) Ernie Shore (1914–17) and Grover Cleveland Alexander, starting pitchers in the opening game of the 1915 World Series.

The pennant winners' .248 team batting average was bettered by three other clubs, and their 550 runs were topped by five other clubs, meaning that it was once again superior pitching that brought Boston its fifth pennant in fourteen years. Larry Gardner's .308 average and 62 runs batted in made him the team leader in each category.

Ruth was now the ace of the staff, with a 23–12 record, leading the league in ERA (1.75) and shutouts (9). Following him were Leonard (18–12), Mays (18–13), Shore (16–10), and Foster (14–7). The 1916 season also saw the sixth and seventh no-hitters in Red Sox history: on June 21 Foster stifled the Yankees, 2–0, at Fenway, and on August 30 Leonard stopped the Browns, 4–0, also at Fenway.

Supporting Boston's tight pitching was the league's best defense: the Sox established an American League record for fewest errors committed (183) and had the highest team fielding average (.972)—the first of a major-league-record six consecutive seasons they finished on top in glove work. The defensive bulwark of the infield was Everett Scott, who, beginning in 1916, led American League shortstops in fielding for an unmatched eight consecutive years (the final two wearing a Yankee uniform).

For the third straight year (following the Braves in 1914 and the Phillies in 1915), the National League had a first-time pennant winner—the Brooklyn Dodgers, managed by Wilbert Robinson. The Dodgers had a couple of strong hitters in first baseman Jake Daubert and outfielder Zack Wheat, each of quiet, reserved personality, quite unlike teammate Casey Stengel, then a twenty-six-year-old outfielder of modest achievements (he batted .279 that year). Even then Stengel was glib and irrepressible. Encountering Shore and Lewis on the field before the opener, Stengel greeted them with a wave of the hand.

"Hello, boys," Casey said. "What do you think your losing share is going to come to?"

"We laughed him off," Shore said. "We didn't think it was possible for anybody to beat us. Our pitching was too good."

Ernie knew what he was talking about, and backed it up himself by winning the opener, 6–5, and the finale, 4–1, as the Red Sox took the Dodgers in five.

Jack Barry (1915–17, 1919). Between the Athletics and Red Sox, he played on six pennant winners in seven years.

Except for Game 2, it was hardly a memorable Series. In the second game, the longest by innings in World Series history, the Red Sox took a fourteen-inning, 2–1 victory. It was the day that Babe Ruth took center stage in a World Series for the first time. Most of Ruth's October heroics would come in a Yankee uniform and be performed at home plate. This time, the young Boston left-hander worked his magic from the mound. After yielding a run to the Dodgers in the top of the first, Ruth put the cork in the bottle.

Boston tied the game in the bottom of the third on Scott's triple and Ruth's ground ball, and then Babe and Brooklyn left-hander Sherry Smith matched zeros until the bottom of the fourteenth, when a pinch-hit single by Del Gainor brought in the winning run. Ruth delivered 13⅓ straight scoreless innings, the first batch of what would become a record 29⅔ consecutive World Series goose eggs, a mark that would stand until 1961.

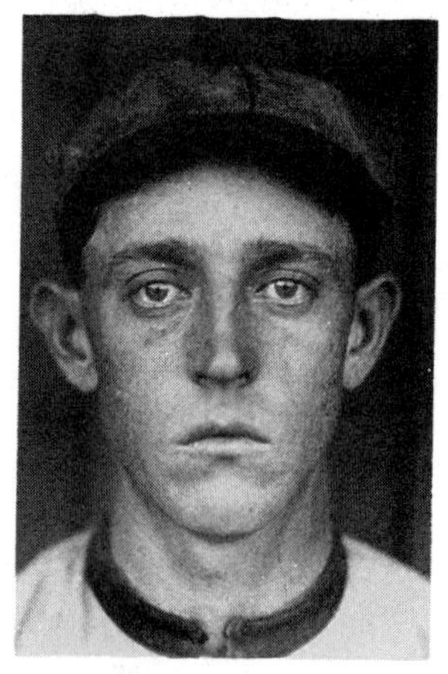
Tilly Walker (1916–17), who had the unenviable job of replacing Tris Speaker in center field.

The Dodgers won Game 3, but Leonard delivered a 6–2 win in Game 4 (helped by Gardner's three-run, inside-the-park homer in the top of the third inning), and then Shore put it to sleep in Game 5. With Boston again playing its Series home games at Braves Field, Game 5 drew a crowd of 42,620, which not only was a new World Series attendance record but also was the largest paying crowd ever to see a baseball game up to that time.

Rumors had been circulating since late in the season that Carrigan was planning to retire, and Bill himself was doing nothing to discourage them. Some people believed this was a ploy to squeeze more money out of Lannin, but others said that such a scheme would be out of character for the skipper. So there was disappointment but not surprise among the Red Sox players when Carrigan announced to them after the final game of the World Series that he was leaving baseball to enter the banking business in his hometown of Lewiston, Maine. The thirty-three-year-old catcher-manager (who had been playing less and less) left behind a managerial record of high achievement: three full seasons that saw one second-place finish, two pennants, and two world championships. His players were sorry to see him go. Ruth, Shore, and many others said in later years that "Rough" was the best manager they had ever played for.

There was another high-echelon departure from Boston baseball that December, as Joseph Lannin decided to sell out his interest in the Red Sox. The team was still a profitable enterprise, but Lannin was being nagged by ill health and also was tired of bickering with the dictatorial Ban Johnson, who continued to run the league he had founded with an iron hand.

Lannin had no trouble finding a buyer. The new man was Harry Frazee, and the best anyone would ever say of him was that he meant well.

Carl Mays (1915–19), who was a 20-game winner for the Red Sox in 1917 and 1918. He was one of the first to be dealt to New York.

Tilly Walker steaming into third on his first-inning triple in the opening game of the 1916 World Series at Braves Field. The third baseman is Mike Mowrey, while the hustling umpire is former Red Sox pitcher Bill Dinneen.

That's manager Carrigan at bat in Game 4 of the 1916 Series, played at Brooklyn's Ebbets Field. Chief Meyers is the catcher, John Quigley the umpire. Notice how Carrigan is choking up on the bat. That was the style for many hitters of that era.

Rube Foster (*left*) and Ernie Shore setting out on a road trip in 1917. (*Courtesy NBL*)

— 4 —

Robbery

Harry Frazee was, by most accounts, a likable man, a convivial companion, with a bit of the rascal's errant charm. On the negative side, we find only one serious failing, and this is more malady than vice: Harry had an unquenchable passion for producing musical comedies on Broadway.

Thirty-six years old when he bought the Red Sox, the plumpish, round-faced Frazee, a native of Peoria, Illinois, was an ambitious man, with dreams of smash hits on Broadway and World Series in Boston. But in trying to achieve the former, he began building a foundation of pure quicksand for the latter. He was the greatest one-man disaster ever to befall any baseball franchise.

With Carrigan gone, the new manager was second baseman Jack Barry, another Holy Cross man. Just thirty years old, Jack had played on four pennant winners with the Athletics and was considered a most studious baseball man. In trying for a third straight pennant, however, Jack and the Red Sox ran into a strong Chicago White Sox team (the same unit that would throw the World Series in 1919) and finished second, nine games out.

The twenty-two-year-old Babe Ruth continued fashioning his image as baseball's burgeoning young superman by excelling both on the mound and at bat. The hard-throwing southpaw was 24–13, completing 35 of his 38 starts and working to a 2.01 ERA. In 123 at-bats, he whaled away at a .325 average, hitting 2 home runs. Combining his on-the-field heroics with that magnetic personality and ingenuous charm, Ruth was now the most popular man in town.

"Walking into a restaurant with him," said Ernie Shore, "was like going in with a brass band. People waved to him and shouted to him and he always responded, yelling back at them, smiling around the big cigar he always had clenched in his teeth."

(Opposite page)
Jack Barry signing his contract to manage the Red Sox in the 1917 season. Seated at the right is Harry Frazee. The gentleman standing is not known.
(Courtesy NBL)

Babe Ruth.

And twenty-game winner or not, there was already talk of getting that big bat into the lineup on a regular basis.

"I remember saying to Barry one day," Hooper recalled. " 'You have a problem,' I told him. 'What's that?' he asked. 'Getting that big monkey's bat into the lineup every day.' He just laughed, but I knew they were already thinking about it, in 1917."

On June 23, Ruth and Shore were involved in one of baseball's all-time pitching oddities. Babe started that afternoon at Fenway against the Washington Senators. He began by walking the lead-off man, Ray Morgan. There were a few close pitches that Ruth thought should have gone his way, and when umpire Brick Owens called the last one ball four, the exasperated southpaw blew his top. Not a retiring type, Owens yelled back, and a moment later Ruth came charging down from the mound, announcing his intention to put a few dents in the umpire's skull. No blows were struck, but Ruth was kicked out of the game.

Barry now had a dilemma: The game had just started, and he was suddenly without a pitcher. So he turned to Shore and told him to get out on the mound and "stall around until I can get somebody warmed up."

Shore couldn't stall for very long—he had to start pitching. On his first delivery, Morgan was thrown out stealing. Shore retired the next two batters, and Barry decided to leave him in.

"I don't believe I threw seventy-five pitches that whole game," Shore recalled in an interview almost sixty years later. "They just kept hitting it right at somebody. They didn't hit but one ball hard and that was in the ninth inning. John Henry, the catcher, lined one on the nose, but right at Duffy Lewis in left field. That was the second out in the ninth. Then Clark Griffith, who was managing Washington, sent a fellow named Mike Menosky in to bat for the pitcher. Griffith was a hard loser, a very hard loser. He didn't want to see me complete that perfect game. So he had Menosky drag a bunt, just to try and break it up. Menosky could run, too. He was fast. He dragged a pretty good bunt past me, but Jack Barry came in and made just a wonderful one-hand stab of the ball, scooped it up and got him at first. That was a good, sharp ending to the game, which I won by a score of four to zero."

Ernie Shore, who teamed with Ruth to pitch baseball's most peculiar perfect game. (*Courtesy NBL*)

It wasn't until after the season that Shore was officially credited with a perfect game.

It was with a largely revamped team that the Red Sox in 1918 took their fourth pennant and fourth World Series in seven years. In January, they acquired first baseman Stuffy McInnis from the Athletics in exchange for catcher Hick Cady, third baseman Larry Gardner, and outfielder Tilly Walker. A lifetime .300 hitter, Stuffy was one of the great fielding first basemen of all time. (In 1921, he set a record by making just one error in 152 games.)

Replacing Gardner at third was Fred Thomas, who had come to Boston in the Speaker deal a few years before. In another transaction with the Athletics, the Sox sent several players and cash to Philadelphia for outfielder Amos Strunk, catcher Wally Schang, and right-hander Joe Bush, who was known as "Bullet Joe" for the high-octane gas he put on his deliveries.

The country had been at war since April 1917, but so far the war had had little effect on baseball. A year later, however, under a "work-or-fight" order issued by the provost marshall, all able-bodied draft-aged men had to either join up or get into a war-related industry. Even though it was declared a nonessential industry, baseball was by now deep enough in the national consciousness to receive dispensation to continue until September 2 before facing the full blast of the draft. (The deadline was further extended to allow the playing of the World Series.)

So it was a shortened schedule in 1918, the only time in its history that baseball has been so interfered with. The Red Sox played just 126 games. (Most of the other clubs averaged about that amount.) Military service cost the Red Sox the services of second baseman–manager Jack Barry; reserve first baseman Dick Hoblitzell; infielders Mike McNally and Hal Janvrin; outfielder Duffy Lewis; and pitchers Ernie Shore, Herb Pennock, and Dutch Leonard (who pitched his second no-hitter on June 3 against Detroit before going off to war).

John ("Stuffy") McInnis (1918–21). Stuffy was a .300 hitter and one of the sharpest fielding first basemen of all time. *(Courtesy NBL)*

Under new manager Ed Barrow, the Sox edged out Cleveland by two and a half games before the curtain came down on September 2 and brought the season to its premature close. Outhit by five other clubs, Boston did it once again on the strength of a strong mound corps, led by submarine-balling right-hander Carl Mays, who was 21–13. A cold, testy character, Mays was never popular with teammates wherever he pitched, but he was always a big winner. On August 30, he pitched Boston to a pair of 12–0 and 4–1 complete-game victories over the Athletics at Fenway, an iron-man stunt that put the Sox within a game of clinching the pennant.

Behind Mays was Sam Jones (16–5), Joe Bush (15–15), and Babe Ruth (13–7). Ruth's win total was lower than usual because by now the great transition was beginning to take place: Babe started 20 games on the mound, 59 in the outfield, and 13 at first base. Getting 317 official at-bats, he batted .300 and won the first of his dozen home-run crowns with 11 long shots (tied with Philadelphia's Tilly Walker). While 11 home runs may be paltry stuff today, they must be viewed in perspective. In 1918, 11 home runs were more than four other *clubs* in the league managed, and the Red Sox themselves only hit a grand total of 15 (including Babe's 11). Boston fans were settling back to enjoy a whole new performance from their favorite player.

The World Series, which began on September 5 in the home field of the National League's pennant-winning Chicago Cubs, was dominated by pitching, which was exceptionally tight on both sides.

Ruth won the opener, 1–0, extending his World Series string of scoreless innings to 22$^{1}/_{3}$. After Bush lost Game 2 by a 3–1 score, Mays put the Sox up a notch with a 2–1 win. Ruth, with ninth-inning help from Bush, took Game 4 by a 3–2 score. By not being scored upon until the top of the eighth, Ruth stretched his scoreless-inning string to 29$^2/_3$, a World Series record that stood until 1961, when it was broken by Yankee left-hander Whitey Ford. After a 3–0 Chicago victory in Game 5, Mays wrapped it up with a 2–1 victory in Game 6.

Wally Schang (1918–20), Boston's sharp-hitting catcher, who was traded to the Yankees. Wally hit over .300 for the Sox in 1919 and 1920.

So Red Sox fans were breathing the rare, sweet air of winners. They had every reason to be proud of their team, which had now won four world championships in seven years. And along with the victories, Red Sox fans had taken pride through the years in claiming as their own some of the game's most luminous stars: Cy Young, Jimmy Collins, Joe Wood, Tris Speaker, and now the greatest of them all, this magnificent young hybrid, Babe Ruth, who, as a twenty-game winner, ERA leader, and home-run champion, was already becoming folklore.

The war was over now and an exultant, self-confident America was gearing up for the most exuberant and madcap decade in its history. But even as baseball-proud New England lay quietly under the snows of winter, there were ominous rumblings in New York.

Colonel Jacob Ruppert (that "Colonel" was an honorary tag laid on the brewery millionaire by a New York governor) had recently bought the Yankees and was determined to turn them into winners—the Yankees had yet to win their first pennant. Toward this end Ruppert was willing to spend money, an intention that always attracts friends and influences people. At the same time, Harry Frazee's treasury was being steadily depleted by his passion for the Broadway stage, upon whose boards his shows were laying a series of ornate eggs. Harry's poor judgment and the upturned noses of the New York critics were slowly and unwittingly conspiring to lay to waste baseball's most successful team.

The first hint of the oncoming riptide of disaster occurred in December 1918, when Frazee sold Ernie Shore, Duffy Lewis, and Dutch Leonard to the Yankees for $15,000 and four players, none of whom was of much help to Boston. Shore and Lewis were near the end of the string, but Leonard was still an effective pitcher. (Dutch wrangled with Ruppert over money and was soon sold to Detroit.)

Del Gainor (1914–17, 1918), Boston's backup first baseman.

The 1919 season proved to be rough sailing for the Red Sox. The club got off to a slow start and never recovered. In mid-July ace right-hander Carl Mays, struggling with a 5–11 record, walked off the mound in the middle of a game, grumbling that his teammates were playing less than enthusiastically behind him and announcing he would never pitch for the Red Sox again.

At the end of the month, Frazee sold Mays to the Yankees for the sizable sum of $40,000. This infuriated Ban Johnson, who suspended the temperamental pitcher. Ruppert, a man whose will was a match for Johnson's, brought a restraining injunction against Johnson, and after some storming about in the courtrooms, Ban backed down and Mays joined the Yankees. This episode rocked the foundation of Johnson's authority and helped pave the way for the appointment, in November 1920, of Judge Kenesaw Mountain Landis as the game's first commissioner and supreme authority.

Despite all the controversy, and despite a disappointing tie for fifth place, 1919 was an exciting year for Red Sox fans, thanks to the record-book slugging of Ruth. With his pitching career now all but behind him (he was 9–5 in 15 starts), Boston's twenty-four-year-old outfielder created some fresh history in the already historic old city on the Charles River. Attacking the ball with an impact never before seen in baseball, Ruth hit a remarkable 29 home runs, more than enough to establish a new major-league record. (This was the last year of the dead ball.) The American League record had been 16, by Socks Seybold for the Athletics in 1902; the National League mark (for the twentieth century), Gavvy Cravath's 24 for the Phillies in 1915. (Playing in a park with foul lines less than 200

feet, an old-timer named Ned Williamson had hit 27 homers for the Chicago White Stockings in 1884.)

(OPPOSITE PAGE) Ed Barrow. (*Courtesy NBL*)

"There's no record like a home-run record," Harry Hooper said. "And not only did Babe break it, but he was hitting them further than anybody thought possible. I remember people saying, 'Twenty-nine home runs! Nobody will ever do that again!' Well, the next year Babe hit fifty-four, and then fifty-nine the year after that. But by then he was in a Yankee uniform."

Yes, the incredible was about to happen. The greatest one-man show in baseball history was about to be swapped for a pile of greenbacks.

Harry Frazee was pinched for money. Jacob Ruppert had lots of it, along with a burning desire to improve his Yankees. Ruth was agitating for a larger contract, one commensurate with his burgeoning stature as a gate attraction (he was earning about $10,000 at the time). Harry Frazee, taking a myopic view of things, saw only one logical thing to do. So that fall, while the Chicago White Sox were scheming to throw the World Series to Cincinnati, Harry was plotting to throw the Red Sox to New York.

Despite the impassioned pleas of manager Ed Barrow, Frazee began laying the groundwork for the deal with Ruppert, whose Yankee offices were virtually next door to Harry's theatrical suite on New York's 42nd Street. Frazee's financial woes were at the point of strangulation. He still owed Lannin money on the purchase of the club, and Lannin was calling in the notes. So Harry was going to need more than the $125,000 Ruppert had agreed to pay for Ruth. Therefore, in addition to the Ruth money, Ruppert agreed to a personal loan of over $300,000 to Frazee, the loan to be secured by a lien on Fenway Park.

The transaction was completed on December 26, 1919, and announced publicly on January 6, 1920. The groans of dismay that rose from New England were drowned out by the shouts of elation from New York. With the lively ball about to come into

Babe Ruth.

play, the Yankees had just taken possession of the most spectacular single force in all sports history, a man who would become the mighty cornerstone of a dynasty that would not run out of energy for more than forty years.

"I believe the sale of Ruth will ultimately strengthen the team," Frazee said, attaining a level of hyperbole not even the most unctuous of politicians would ever have dared attempt.

— 5 —

In the Wilderness

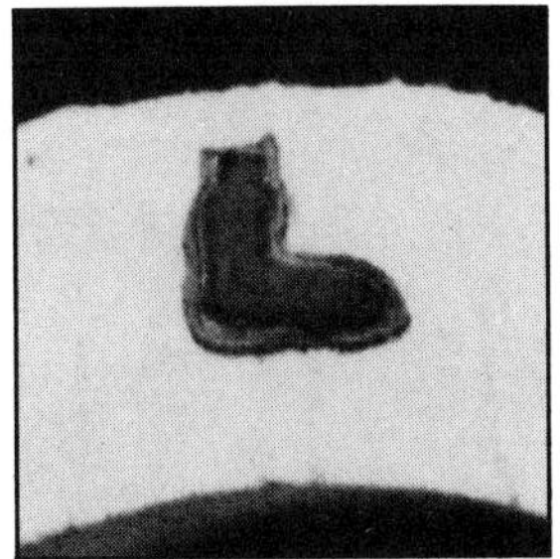

RED SOX

And so began the Boston Red Sox' long, gloomy wandering through the baseball wilderness. While the rest of the country spent the 1920s in a prolonged postwar binge, while American sports went rousingly through a golden age, while Babe Ruth and his former Red Sox teammates led the Yankees to six pennants, the Red Sox went nowhere.

Had Harry Frazee gone off and become a tree in Idaho, the Red Sox might have survived the Ruth deal, for the club still had some excellent talent, particularly on the mound in right-handers Sam Jones, Joe Bush, Waite Hoyt, and the superb left-hander Herb Pennock. They also had the quick-fingered Everett Scott at shortstop and .300-hitting Wally Schang behind the plate. But Frazee stayed in Boston, even as his shows turned into corpses on Broadway, and his debts continued to mount.

Boston finished fifth in 1920. In the spring of 1921, the last of the great outfield triumvirate departed—though not for cash—when Hooper was traded to the White Sox for first baseman–outfielder Shano Collins and outfielder Nemo Leibold.

"Frazee did me a favor," Hooper said. "I was glad to get away from that graveyard."

Also leaving was manager Ed Barrow; he, too, went off to join the Yankees, as general manager. His replacement was an old Boston (National League) hero, Hugh Duffy. An outfielder in the 1890s, Duffy had in 1894 posted baseball's most astronomical batting average—.438. Running the club in 1921 and 1922, he finished fifth and then last.

In December 1920, Waite Hoyt, Wally Schang, and two lesser players were traded to New York for four players, including catcher Muddy Ruel, a talented player who was later traded to Washington.

Sam Jones won 23 for the Sox in 1921 and Joe Bush 16, which in those days was enough to earn a fellow a ticket to New

(OPPOSITE PAGE) Hugh Duffy, who once hit .438 in the National League. He managed the Red Sox in 1921 and 1922, without much success.

York. So on December 21, Jones, Bush, and Everett Scott were traded to the Yankees for four players, and although no cash was announced as part of either of the last two transactions, one suspects that Ruppert's checkbook did not lie idly by.

On July 23, 1922, the Red Sox sent third baseman Joe Dugan and outfielder Elmer Smith to the Yankees for four players and $50,000. The Yankees at the time were in a bruising pennant battle with the St. Louis Browns, who complained so bitterly over the timing of the deal that Commissioner Landis established the June 15 trading deadline.

Waite Hoyt (1919–20). He was so young when he came to the big leagues that they called him "Schoolboy." He was just 6–6 in 1920, the year before the Yankees bought him. But the New Yorkers knew what they were doing. The twenty-one-year-old Hoyt immediately became an ace pitcher. *(Courtesy NBL)*

It was rumored at the time that Ruppert and his colleagues were avid readers of the reviews of Frazee's new shows, quickly turning to the Red Sox roster to see whom next to pluck. After the 1922 season, there wasn't much, except for one last jewel—Herb Pennock. And so, on January 30, 1923, the Yankees completed the Rape of the Red Sox with the acquisition of Pennock, for whom they gave Frazee three nondescript players and a check for $50,000.

The decline that had begun with the eighth-place finish in 1922 continued until 1933. In those twelve moribund years, the Red Sox finished sixth once, seventh twice, and eighth nine times. (It was, of course, an eight-team league at that time.)

Adding greater darkness to Boston's eclipse were the sensational exploits of Ruth and all those one-time Red Sox pitchers now in Yankee pinstripes. Bush, Mays, Jones, Hoyt, and Pennock were each twenty-game winners in New York, with the latter two having long, Hall of Fame careers.

With the team playing dismally, Red Sox fans had to content themselves with the occasional outstanding individual performer or performance. On September 7, 1923, right-hander Howard Ehmke no-hit the Athletics, 4–0. A quality pitcher, Ehmke, who was a 20-game winner in 1923, had been acquired from Detroit in one of Frazee's rare good trades. In his next start after his no-hitter, on September 11, Ehmke one-hit the Yankees, the lone hit being made by Yankee leadoff-man

(TOP LEFT)
Shano Collins (1921–25). He managed the team in 1931 and part of 1932.

(TOP RIGHT)
Joe Bush (1918–21) was 16–9 for Boston in 1921, which in those years was the same as buying a ticket for New York.

(BOTTOM LEFT)
The best of the many star pitchers who went from Boston to New York was Herb Pennock (1915–17, 1919–22, 1934).

(BOTTOM RIGHT)
Sam Jones (1916–21). Sam was 23–16 for Boston in 1921. The next year he was pitching for the Yankees. *(Courtesy NBL)*

Whitey Witt. It was a bad-hop single, and as the game progressed some of the Boston writers asked the official scorer to change it to an error. The scorer refused, although conceding that if it had come late in the game he might have scored it an error. The hotly debated hit cost Ehmke the distinction of being the first man to pitch back-to-back no-hitters. (Johnny Vander Meer, who did it for Cincinnati in 1938, remains the only man to have achieved this feat.)

In July 1923, there was an announcement that caused Red Sox fans to shake their heads philosophically: Frazee had sold the club to Bob Quinn, formerly an executive with the Browns. Coincidentally, this was the year that the Yankees won their third straight pennant but their first World Series. Morosely, Red Sox followers were able to count eleven former Boston players on the world champions' roster.

(A final note on the bumbling Frazee: He never gave up on Broadway, and in 1925 his persistence was rewarded when he produced *No, No, Nanette,* a smash hit with a lovely score by Vincent Youmans, including the lilting "Tea for Two," which earned him buckets of money and has become part of the theatrical repertory. Unfortunately, Harry had just a few years to enjoy his success; he died in 1929 at the age of forty-eight.

One thing that last-place teams breed is new managers, and the Red Sox had their share during their long, dark night. In 1923, Duffy was replaced by Frank Chance, of Tinker-to-Evers-to-Chance fame. Frank lasted one year. Quinn then brought in Lee Fohl, who had previously managed the Indians and Browns. He lasted three years. Then, in 1927, the club sought to rub an old magic lamp by bringing back Bill Carrigan. Bill, who could do nothing but win during his first tenure, this time did nothing but lose, suffering three last-place finishes in 1927, 1928, and 1929. (In 1927, Red Sox fans watched wistfully while Ruth smashed 8 of his record 60 homers at Fenway Park.) Carrigan was replaced in 1930 by Heinie Wagner, shortstop of the 1912 world champions, but

(TOP LEFT)
Howard Ehmke won 20 for the Red Sox in 1923. Ehmke (1923–26) was the club's last 20-game winner until 1935.

(TOP RIGHT)
Boston's manager in 1923 was Frank Chance, one-time infield partner of Tinker and Evers.

(BOTTOM LEFT)
Outfielder Ira Flagstead (1923–29). He batted .311 in 1923 and .305 the next year.
(Courtesy NBL)

(BOTTOM RIGHT)
One of the outstanding first basemen of his era, George Burns played for Boston in 1922–23, batting .306 and .328.
(Courtesy NBL)

Heinie saw no daylight either and in 1931 was canned in favor of Shano Collins, who lasted into the 1932 season when he was excused in favor of utility infielder Marty McManus, who lasted through the 1933 season.

Collins and McManus bore the burden of the team's worst season in 1932: 43–111, a record that was rewarded with the franchise's lowest-ever attendance, 182,150.

Now and then during those years, a player of genuine talent slipped into a Red Sox uniform. Perhaps the most notable of these strangers was Charlie ("Red") Ruffing, a big right-hander who threw the ball hard. The talented Ruffing did his best in Boston but had little to show for it. Joining the club at

First baseman–outfielder Joe ("Moon") Harris (1922–25). Joe hit .300 wherever he played and for Boston he turned in averages of .316, .335, and .301.

Lee Fohl (*left*), who managed the Red Sox from 1924 to 1926, is shown here with Yankee skipper Miller Huggins.

the tail end of 1924, Red was a regular starter for the next five years, compiling a 39–93 record, including league-leading loss totals in 1928 (25) and 1929 (22). Nevertheless, the Yankees liked what they saw, and on May 6, 1930, in a deal that no doubt evoked some bad old memories among Sox fans, Red was spirited onto baseball's version of the Underground Railroad and sent to New York for $50,000 and outfielder Cedric Durst. Once in a Yankee suit, Red unlimbered and became a big and steady winner—his Yankee record was 231–124.

Phil Todt (1924–30), Boston's regular first baseman throughout most of the 1920s. Phil's best was .278 in 1925.

In May 1927, the Red Sox engineered a steal of a deal of their own when they lassoed young infielder Buddy Myer from Washington for shortstop Topper Rigney, who had just about topped out a so-so career. Buddy batted .281 in 1927 and .313 in 1928, whereupon Boston unaccountably traded him back to Washington for a parcel of players who added little to Boston baseball lore. Myer became a perennial .300-hitting second baseman for Washington for the next dozen years, winning the batting crown in 1935.

Playing second base for the Red Sox from 1926 to 1930 was Bill Regan. His high was .288 in 1929.

In 1931, Boston's journeyman outfielder Earl Webb put himself in the record books when he hit an all-time-high 67 doubles to go along with a .333 batting average. This remains one of baseball's curious records—a significant offensive mark held by a player who is almost totally unknown to the average fan. Webb was traded to Detroit the following year and by 1934 was gone from the majors, leaving behind a seven-year average of .306.

In 1932, the Red Sox had their first batting champion in Dale Alexander. A big, slow-footed first baseman, Alexander was obtained from Detroit on June 12 along with outfielder Roy Johnson for Webb. Alexander, who had hit .343, .326, and .325 for Detroit in the three preceding years, had played in just twenty-three games in 1932, batting .250. Once traded to Boston, however, he caught fire and began whaling away, hitting at a .372 clip. His combined average of .367 was good enough to lead the league, making him the first man ever to win a batting

Red Ruffing (1924–30).

(TOP LEFT)
Buddy Myer (1927–28), the superb infielder the Red Sox had and let get away. He batted .313 in 1928.

(TOP RIGHT)
Jack Rothrock (1925–32), a versatile man who played every infield and outfield position. He batted .300 in 1929.
(Courtesy NBL)

(BOTTOM LEFT)
Johnnie Heving (1924–25, 1928–30), a backup catcher for the Red Sox. He hit .319 as a part-timer in 1929.
(Courtesy NBL)

(BOTTOM RIGHT)
A somewhat serious appearance earned Danny MacFayden the nickname "Deacon Danny." MacFayden (1926–32) was 16–12 for a dismal Red Sox club in 1931.
(Courtesy NBL)

title while playing for two different clubs in the same year. But then injuries slowed him down, and after batting .281 in 1933 he was dropped.

The Red Sox may have been late bloomers when it came to winning a batting title, but they have since become baseball's most prolific winners in this glamour category, capturing twenty more titles.

The year 1932 signaled rock bottom for the Red Sox. This was the year the club lost 111 games and attendance dropped to under 200,000. The nadir was reached in May and June, when the team won nine and lost forty-four. Though he had struggled long and honorably to keep his team afloat, Bob Quinn, with no personal fortune to sustain him, was finally forced to sell out. In February 1933, a disappointed but greatly relieved Quinn sold the team to a thirty-year-old multimillionaire named Thomas Austin Yawkey.

Right-hander Jack Russell (1926–32, 1936). He was one of Boston's better starting pitchers, but usually in a lost cause. Note the sock emblem on his cap.
(*Courtesy NBL*)

(TOP LEFT)
Tom Oliver (1930–33). He was considered one of the top defensive center fielders of his time. His entire four-year major-league career was spent with Boston. In 1,931 official times at bat, he never hit a home run.
(Courtesy NBL)

(TOP RIGHT)
Earl Webb (1930–32), the man who hit all those doubles.
(Courtesy NBL)

It's April 13, 1933, opening day at Yankee Stadium, and some heavy timber is getting together. *Left to right:* Lou Gehrig, Smead Jolley, Babe Ruth, and Dale Alexander. Jolley (1932–33) was a good hitter but weak fielder. Alexander (1932–33) was the first Red Sox player to win a batting title.
(Courtesy NBL)

(Left)
Harold ("Rabbit") Warstler (1930–33), a light-hitting utility infielder.
(*Courtesy NBL*)

(Right)
Marty McManus (1931–33), veteran American League infielder who was Boston's player-manager in 1932 and 1933.
(*Courtesy NBL*)

— 6 —

Winds of Change

He took over the Red Sox in 1933, and by the time he died in 1976, Tom Yawkey had become as much a part of New England baseball history as Fenway Park itself. Millionaire though he was, Yawkey possessed in abundance what is best described as "the common touch." He was unpretentious, never flaunting his wealth; he loved his team dearly and was sentimental about his players (going quietly into his pocket to help some who were in postcareer need), rooting for them with the same fervor as any bleacher fan—and fan he was, with enough boy in him to occasionally keep the Fenway lights burning after a game and go down to home plate with bat in hand and take aim at his left-field wall. He was, in short, a regular guy.

The new owner of the Red Sox was described by one Boston paper as a "financier-sportsman." His money was inherited; his love of baseball was innate. He was the nephew and later adopted son of Bill Yawkey, who had once owned the Detroit Tigers and who left young Tom an inheritance of more than $3 million. Tom's mother (Bill's sister) left him even more, and still more came from his grandfather, who had had extensive holdings in lumber and ore.

Unlike some men of many dollars, Yawkey was a man of few words, and among the few that he spoke upon taking over the team were these: "I don't intend to mess with a loser."

The new owner's first move was a shrewd one—he hired as the team's vice-president and general manager one of baseball's all-time great players and one of its finest intellects, Eddie Collins. An active player for a quarter of a century with the Philadelphia Athletics and Chicago White Sox, during which time he built his reputation as baseball's premier second baseman, Collins had been serving as Connie Mack's top lieutenant. With Mack's blessings, Eddie left Philadelphia and joined Tom Yawkey and the Red Sox.

Yawkey had promised to spend whatever was necessary to build the Sox back into a winning team, and he wasn't long in

(OPPOSITE PAGE) Tom Yawkey.

translating that promise into action. Guided by Collins, Yawkey flapped his checkbook early in the 1933 season—in those depression-dark days it made a most seductive sound—and purchased catcher Rick Ferrell from the St. Louis Browns (whose attendance for the entire *season* was just over 88,000). Ferrell was an excellent catcher and a .300 hitter. A few days later, on May 12, Boston reversed an old trend by buying for $100,000 two players from the Yankees: pitcher George Pipgras and third baseman Billy Werber. Werber was a good, hustling player who in 1934 and 1935 led the league in stolen bases, only the second Red Sox player ever to lead in this department. Pipgras, however, soon came down with an arm injury and never really helped.

Roy Johnson (1932–35), hard-hitting outfielder who batted over .300 three times for the Red Sox, with a high of .320 in 1934.

Boston climbed out of the cellar in Yawkey's first year, finishing seventh: dubious progress, true, but a move in the right direction.

The Philadelphia Athletics, with a truly mighty team, had won pennants in 1929, 1930, and 1931. But now Connie Mack was experiencing a common 1930s' woe—financial pressure. A combination of high-salaried players and declining attendance was forcing the A's owner-manager to begin selling off his stars. On December 12, 1933, Mack sold his great catcher Mickey Cochrane to Detroit for $100,000, and on the same day dispatched baseball's reigning king of pitchers, Lefty Grove, to the Red Sox, along with left-hander Rube Walberg and second baseman Max Bishop, for $125,000.

Billy Werber (1933–36), Boston's hustling third baseman. He led the league in stolen bases in 1934 and 1935 and again in 1937. He batted .321 for Boston in 1934. (*Courtesy NBL*)

It was a stunning deal. A twenty-game winner during each of the seven previous years (including 31 wins in 1931), the thirty-three-year-old Grove possessed creation's most sizzling fastball, with a temperament to match. Explosive in defeat ("He lost so seldom," one writer said, "he didn't know how to cope with it."), Lefty was not shy about rearranging clubhouses and berating teammates for lack of support. On one occasion, after a tough loss, he refused to sit with his colleagues on the team bus, choosing instead to walk the five miles back to the hotel. Nevertheless, he was an adored character, his teammates in awe of his talent as well as what has been described as his "terrifying will to win." (Neither Walberg nor Bishop contributed much to Red Sox success over the next few years, both men having seen their best days.)

The much-traveled Lyn Lary, who was Boston's shortstop in 1934.

The whopping Grove transaction did not pay immediate dividends, however, as the great left-hander quickly came down with a sore arm. An embarrassed Connie Mack offered to refund Yawkey's money. It was a gracious gesture and Yawkey was duly appreciative, but the Boston owner said the deal would stand. Grove struggled through an 8–8 season and a 6.50 ERA.

On May 25, 1934, Yawkey sent $25,000 and two players to Cleveland for outfielder Dick Porter and right-hander Wes Ferrell. Brother of Boston's catcher Rick, Wes was in some

Lefty Grove (1934–41).

Boston's brother battery: catcher Rick Ferrell (*left*) and brother Wes. Rick (1933–37) hit .312 in 1936, while Wes (1934–37) was a 25-game winner as well as a .300 hitter.

aspects a mirror image of his hero, Lefty Grove. Wes could be Vesuvian of temperament when the tides were running against him; he had been known to grind his wristwatch to powder under his heel, chew on his glove, punch his own fist into his own jaw, and perform other impromptu rituals while trying to ease the pangs of adversity. But like Grove, Wes had been a winner, opening his major-league career with four straight twenty-victory seasons, an achievement still unequaled. And, like Grove, he had had a sore arm rob him of his good fastball. When the handsome, twenty-six-year-old arrived in Boston, he was getting by on guile and control. His first year he racked up a 14–5 record.

In addition to being a winner on the mound, Ferrell was also one of the great hitting pitchers of all time—he still holds the American League home-run-hitting records for pitchers for a season (9) and a career (36). One of Wes's cherished moments came when he pinch-hit a home run in the bottom of the ninth at Fenway to win a game for his idol, Grove, who was sitting in the clubhouse, assuming his game was lost. When Grove heard what had happened, he took a bottle of wine from his locker and rolled it across the floor to Ferrell.

"At the end of the season," Ferrell said, "I brought it back to Carolina with me and let it sit up on the mantel. It sat up there for years and years. Every time I looked at it I thought of Old Left."

Bucky Harris, Red Sox manager in 1934.

With new manager Bucky Harris running the club in 1934, the Sox climbed to fourth place with a 76–76 record, their first visit to the first division since the pennant year of 1918. Playing in a reconstructed Fenway Park, the improved club saw attendance jump from 1933's 268,715 to 610,640. The single biggest crowd ever to jam into Fenway showed up on August 12, 1934, to watch a doubleheader with the Yankees. But it was more than just this attractive set of games that drew the 41,766 people who filled every seat and clogged the aisles and ramps and stood behind ropes in the outfield. They had come to say farewell to the thirty-nine-year-old Babe Ruth, who, they sensed correctly, was playing his final year with the Yankees.

"It was an emotional day," Wes Ferrell recalled. "The Babe had begun up there and, Yankee or not, he was still in the hearts of the Boston fans. They cheered everything he did. He always loved Fenway Park and the people there, and they showed him that day that it was mutual."

Despite his good showing, Harris was let go after the 1934 season, thanks to another colossal burst of largesse from Yawkey's checkbook. Determined to bring some hard-nosed on-the-field leadership to the club, Yawkey bought Joe Cronin from Washington. The price was $250,000. Cronin was not only a hard-hitting shortstop and manager of the Senators, he was also the son-in-law of club owner Clark Griffith. It had been said of the tight-fisted Griffith that he would have sold his mother, if the price was right. Well, it wasn't his mother, but the price was right for a son-in-law. Even at that staggering (for the time) figure, Yawkey had to cajole Griffith into the deal, with Griff muttering all the way to the bank that "no ballplayer is worth that kind of money." (Griffith was genuinely fond of Cronin, who was not only an exemplary son-in-law but also the heart of the ball club. But a quarter of a million dollars in depression-blighted America was more than a man could resist.)

Mexican-born outfielder Mel Almada (1933–37). His best year in Boston was .290 in 1935. (*Courtesy NBL*)

A handsome, lantern-jawed San Francisco Irishman, Cronin was one of the great hitting shortstops of all time. Defensively, he was mediocre. (On one occasion at Fenway, Joe went down on one knee for a ninth-inning ground ball, muffed it, and allowed the winning runs to score. Grove was on the mound. After the game, according to one Red Sox player, "Joe lit out for the clubhouse, ran into his office and locked the door. He knew what was coming. Well, there was a screen on top of the office wall and Grove pushed a bench against the wall, got up on it and began screaming through that screen down at Joe, telling him that Joe had played like a girl and wasn't good enough for a high school team. Cronin never said a word. He knew Lefty. The next day they were pals again.")

Cronin, who developed a warm personal relationship with Yawkey, was destined to manage the Red Sox longer than any other man—thirteen years. Upon leaving the dugout, he moved into the front office as general manager, and later became president of the American League. Cronin's remains one of the fullest and most distinguished careers in baseball.

Despite the addition of Cronin and a 25–14 record from Ferrell (who also batted .347) and a 20–12 mark from a restored Grove (who led the league with a 2.70 ERA), the Red Sox finished fourth again in 1935. The league at that time had two extremely powerful teams—the Tigers, who won the pennant, and the Yankees, who finished three games behind. Pitching, the pride and joy of Boston's previous pennant winners, was settling in to become the bugaboo of the heavy-hitting teams Yawkey was putting together. After Ferrell and Grove, no Red Sox pitcher won more than ten games in 1935.

(OPPOSITE PAGE) Joe Cronin (1935–45) and Tom Yawkey during spring training, 1935.

One of Boston's 1935 losses involved an unforgettable example of "heads-up" baseball. Playing Cleveland at Fenway on

September 7, the Sox were trailing, 5–1, in the bottom of the ninth, when they launched a rally that scored two runs and had the bases loaded with none out. Cronin was at bat, facing right-hander Oral Hildebrand.

Joe got his pitch and ripped a scorching line drive down the third-base line. The ball was hit so hard that Cleveland third baseman Odell Hale could not get his glove up in time. The ball hit him square in the forehead and caromed through the air to shortstop Bill Knickerbocker, who flipped it to second baseman Roy Hughes, who stepped on second to double up Billy Werber and then fired to first baseman Hal Trosky, who tripled up Mel Almada, the baserunner there. The stunned, embarrassed Hale was then congratulated by his teammates for "using his head" to start a triple play.

The year 1936 saw the New York Yankees begin a run of four straight pennants and four straight world championships. This was a brute-force, juggernaut of a team that would not be

Lefty Grove greeting his former manager, Connie Mack.

beaten. With a lineup that included Joe DiMaggio, Bill Dickey, Lou Gehrig, Joe Gordon, Red Rolfe, Tommy Henrich, George Selkirk, and others, plus a deep and efficient pitching staff, they tore through the league with pennant-winning margins of nineteen, thirteen, nine and a half, and seventeen games. There was no stopping them, though Tom Yawkey certainly tried.

Joe Cronin. Joe's best average in Boston was .325 in 1938.

In December 1935, Yawkey dented his bank account once more, this time for $150,000, with which he induced Connie Mack to part with first baseman Jimmie Foxx and right-hander Johnny Marcum. Marcum, a 17-game winner in 1935, was a disappointment for Boston, but Jimmie Foxx was never a disappointment anywhere.

The twenty-eight-year-old Foxx was the game's most devastating right-handed power hitter, a man who had already won a Triple Crown and two Most Valuable Player Awards and who had hit 58 home runs in 1932. Bringing his compact, power-laden swing to Fenway, the muscular Foxx, who had a physique that looked as though it had been quarried, was immediately hailed as a threat to Ruth's single-season homer record of 60.

Outfielder Doc Cramer (1936–40), one of the most consistent players of his time. He played five years in Boston, hit just one home run but batted over .300 four times.

The tales of Foxx's long-distance hitting were already part of baseball lore. "He could hit a ball as far as anybody," White Sox pitcher Ted Lyons said. "I don't know which stories in particular you've heard about his power hitting, but I'd say you wouldn't go far wrong if you believed them all."

Jimmie was the archetypal Fenway hitter: right-handed and immensely strong. But so strong, according to one teammate, that Fenway was irrelevant, and sometimes even posed a barrier. Center fielder Doc Cramer, whom Yawkey bought from the Athletics in January 1936 for $75,000, said, "That wall meant nothing to Jimmie. When he hit one, it was gone, no matter the park. The wall, in fact, cost him some home runs. Some of his line drives were just beginning to rise when they hit that wall. Those balls would have been home runs in any other park; in Fenway they were doubles, sometimes singles."

BOSTON

(OPPOSITE PAGE)
It's December 1935, and Jimmie Foxx has just been traded from the Athletics to the Red Sox. *(Courtesy NBL)*

In 1936, Foxx batted .338, with 41 home runs and 143 RBIs. Over the six full years he played in Boston, Jimmie paid a solid return on Yawkey's investment, averaging 40 home runs for each of his first five seasons before tapering off to 19 in 1941, his last full summer in Boston. In 1938, he gave the Sox a truly mammoth year, hitting 50 home runs (second in the league to Hank Greenberg's 58) and leading with a .349 batting average and 175 RBIs (fourth highest single-season total in history). The home run and RBI figures remain all-time Red Sox highs. Jimmie won MVP honors for the third time, becoming the first Red Sox player to be so designated. (Of Jimmie's 50 homers in 1938, 35 were struck at Fenway, a club record.)

Late in his career, the ever-smiling, always amiable Foxx ("the most well-liked man in baseball," one writer described him) began developing the drinking problem that would bedevil him for the rest of his life. After leaving baseball in 1945, Foxx moved from one job to another, both in and out of the game. Because of who he was and because people liked him, he had no trouble finding employment. But invariably his weakness for liquor would impair and disable him, and he would move on. Always the sentimentalist and always particularly fond of Jimmie, Tom Yawkey quietly helped Foxx during these last, sad years, until the former slugger died in 1967, at the age of fifty-nine.

Despite the addition of Foxx and a 20–15 season from Ferrell, the Sox finished a disappointing sixth in 1936. Even with his winning season, Wes was providing as many headaches as joys. On August 21, he stormed off the mound at Yankee Stadium in the sixth inning, furious with what he deemed the shabby support behind him. He had done the same thing in his previous start and earlier in the season had thumbed his nose at some loud-mouthed fans in Fenway. This latest episode outraged Cronin, and the skipper immediately suspended his volatile ace and fined him $1,000, a hefty piece of money at the time.

When he learned of Cronin's actions that evening, Wes announced to a New York newspaperman that he was going to "slug that damned Irishman right on his lantern jaw." Never one to back away from anyone, Cronin announced where his jaw would be and when, but by then Ferrell, as he always did, had calmed down. Wes went on to win his 20 games and lead the league with 301 innings pitched, but by now his days in Boston were being counted off by Yawkey and Cronin. The following June, Wes and his brother Rick (a most reserved gentleman) were traded to Washington for outfielder Ben Chapman and right-hander Bobo Newsom.

Moe Berg (1935–39), backup catcher. Moe, who played very little, was known as baseball's most erudite man, one who was fluent in eleven languages—and who couldn't hit the curve ball in any of them. He is rumored to have performed some feats of derring-do as an OSS agent in World War II.

What the Sox had done was trade one headache for two. Newsom was a talented right-hander who was traded or released fifteen times during his long career, usually because he got under somebody's skin, most often the manager's. Bobo was not explosive the way Grove and Ferrell were; he was a most singular character, colorful, witty, and independent. Whenever Cronin walked over from his position during a game to impart some managerial wisdom to Newsom on the art of pitching, the big right-hander would stare disdainfully at him and ask, "Who's telling Old Bobo how to pitch?" Old Bobo lasted until the end of the season and then was traded to the Browns for outfielder Joe Vosmik.

Chapman was another independent thinker, which may work fine in tennis or golf, but when you are playing a team sport like baseball, it means you had better keep your bags packed. Ben had already been dealt away from the Yankees (where as a young player he had advised an aging Babe Ruth to retire before he got hurt, as this was no game "for an old man"), and now Washington was only too happy to be rid of him.

Johnny Marcum (1936–38). The Red Sox expected big things from him when they obtained him from the Athletics, but the best he could do was 13–11 in 1937. (*Courtesy NBL*)

So Ben was dispatched to the care of Joe Cronin, a consummate professional. Joe got the news about Ben one day when he ordered him to bunt, only to see the sign ignored and a double play ensue. When the incensed skipper demanded an explanation, Ben said, "I don't bunt." So, after the 1938 season, despite

Boston's official contingent meeting Judge Landis (*second from left*) in New York during the 1936 World Series between the Yankees and Giants. *Left to right:* Eddie Collins, Landis, Tom Yawkey, and Joe Cronin.

Pinky Higgins taking batting practice at Boston's spring camp at Sarasota, Florida, in March 1937. The catcher is Johnny Peacock. Higgins (1937–38, 1946), who later managed the club, batted over .300 in 1937–38, driving in 106 runs each year.

a .340 batting average, Ben began receiving his mail in Cleveland.

The 1937 Red Sox finished fifth, a step up. The lineup featured four .300 hitters in Cronin, Chapman, Cramer, and new third baseman Pinky Higgins, who had been obtained from the A's for Billy Werber, who had rubbed Cronin the wrong way. "He's too damned intelligent to be a ballplayer," the skipper groused one day. (Werber had graduated with honors from Duke. A stickler for correct language, Werber allegedly lectured a teammate who had yelled on a pop fly, "I got it!" that proper usage was, "I have it.")

Left-hander Fritz Ostermueller (1934–40), whose best year at Fenway was 1938, when he was 13–5. (*Courtesy NBL*)

Despite the various problems Cronin had with individual players, his biggest headache was caused by the Yankees, who kept bringing in gifted young players from their farm system and winning pennants and world championships with an ease and a regularity that had turned them into baseball's aristocracy.

In 1938, the Red Sox outhit the Yankees by 25 points—.299 to .274—but finished in second place (their best windup since 1918), nine and a half games behind the New Yorkers. Jimmie Foxx had his Triple Crown year, Chapman batted .340; Vosmik, .324; Cronin, .325; Higgins, .303; Cramer, .301; and rookie second baseman Bobby Doerr, .289. (Higgins, over a pair of doubleheaders on June 21–22, had rapped out twelve straight hits, bettering by one the record set by Speaker in 1920.) The difference between the two clubs lay in power and pitching: New York hit 174 home runs; Boston, 98 (50 of them by Foxx). New York's four top starters had a combined 69–31 record; Boston's were 57–35.

Ben Chapman (1937–38).

In one sense, the 1938 club marked the end of an era in Red Sox history, though not because something was particularly ending but because something was about to significantly begin. The 1938 club, with one notable exception, would soon go asunder. Foxx had several good years left, but Cramer, Chapman, Vosmik, and Higgins would soon be going elsewhere.

(TOP LEFT)
Catcher Gene Desautels (1937–40). He batted .291 in 1938, the year he did the bulk of the catching for Boston. *(Courtesy NBL)*

(TOP RIGHT)
He played just about everywhere else, and in 1937 Bobo Newsom was with the Red Sox.

(BOTTOM LEFT)
Right-hander Jack Wilson (1935–41). He was 16–10 in 1937, his best year.

(BOTTOM RIGHT)
Bobby Doerr (1937–44, 1946–51), the Red Sox' all-time second baseman.

Pinky Higgins rapping out his record twelfth consecutive hit on June 21, 1938.

Grove was still winning—14–4 in 1938 and for the eighth time the league's ERA leader—but Lefty was now thirty-eight years old and pitching less and less.

The notable exception was second baseman Bobby Doerr, a twenty-year-old rookie who that year was beginning the career that would eventually earn him the accolade as Boston's finest second baseman ever. By far the youngest player in a starting lineup that averaged twenty-nine years of age, Doerr broke in with a .289 batting average and 80 RBIs and quickly earned a name for his superb glovework.

The following year, the Sox would introduce into their lineup another twenty-year-old. This one would bring to baseball the purest power swing in its history and to Red Sox fans a pride they had not felt since the brief Boston heyday of Babe Ruth. It was Ted Williams's arrival that automatically divided the eras of Boston baseball. There is the pre-Williams era and the post-Williams era, and in between was the greatest hitter the game has ever seen.

(TOP LEFT)
Joe Vosmik (1938–39). In 1938, he batted .324 and led the league with 201 hits.
(Courtesy NBL)

(TOP RIGHT)
Jim Bagby, Jr. (1938–40, 1946). Jim, whose father was a 31-game winner for Cleveland in 1920, did half as well for Boston, going 15–11 in 1938.

(BOTTOM LEFT)
Right-hander Emerson Dickman (1936, 1938–41). He did most of his work out of the bullpen.
(Courtesy NBL)

(BOTTOM RIGHT)
Joe Cronin.
(Courtesy NBL)

Jimmie Foxx (1936–42). His 50 home runs and 175 runs batted in in 1938 remain Red Sox club records. Jimmie autographed this picture to Eddie Collins.

— 7 —

Teddy Ballgame

BOS

Boston had seen great players before, but not without a mingling of pride and pain. Speaker had been sold to Cleveland, Ruth to New York. Grove and Foxx would loom larger in baseball history as Athletics than as Red Sox. But Ted Williams—well, he came to Boston and he stayed. He played for a long time and he played nowhere else, in no other uniform. To Red Sox fans, he was their own, uniquely their own.

Williams was a creature of baseball unlike any who had ever played. All men came to the game to succeed; some strove purposefully to star, a few to dominate. Only Williams came with the soaring ambition to be the greatest hitter that ever lived. It was no vague, adolescent fancy carried over into young manhood; with Williams, it was dead-serious, almost spiritual, and never in his mind unattainable. There was nothing arrogant either in his goal or in his determination to achieve it; on the contrary, what he wanted for himself was wholly admirable, and no man ever worked in a batter's box harder or with more scholarly intensity.

Nature had conspired with him. No hitter ever came to the plate with a greater arsenal. He was tall and strong, gifted with remarkable eyesight, reflexes, judgment, self-discipline, hand-eye coordination. He would not, even for one pitch, be deterred from what he was about; he would not swing at a ball that was not a strike, and he had microscopic knowledge of the strike zone—to the extent that umpires often deferred to his judgment on a close pitch. His swing was never tentative; he never moved the bat unless it was going all the way around. The swing had a wicked snap to it, and it was aesthetically perfect. All hitting before him led up to the peak of Williams; all hitting since has trailed down from him.

The prospector responsible for bringing this nugget to Boston was Eddie Collins. Eddie was on a scouting trip to San Diego in 1936, expressly to size up the club's second baseman,

(OPPOSITE PAGE)
Ted Williams (1939–42, 1946–60) in 1939, his rookie year.
(Courtesy NBL)

Bobby Doerr, on whom the Sox had taken an option. Collins liked what he saw of Doerr and exercised the option. He also liked what he saw of a tall, lanky seventeen-year-old who was in the batting cage demonstrating the swing he had so tirelessly perfected on the playgrounds of his native San Diego. The boy was in his first year of pro ball. He played in 42 games, batted .271, hit no home runs. But statistics were irrelevant to Collins; all Eddie saw was that swing, the swing that would soon mesmerize America's game and make Williams the most riveting at-bat since Ruth.

The greatest one-two punch in Red Sox history: Jimmie Foxx (*left*) and Ted Williams. (*Courtesy NBL*)

Collins obtained an option on Williams's contract. In 1937, Ted's first full year of pro ball, he batted .291 and hit 23 home runs. A year later, he was in Boston's spring camp, brash and self-confident, ready to crash an outfield that consisted of a trio of .300-hitting veterans—Cramer, Chapman, and Vosmik.

Outfielder–first baseman Lou Finney (1939–45). He batted .320 in 1940.

"We'd never seen a rookie like him," Cramer said. "He was cocky, fidgety, and he wised-off a lot. But you had to like him. Ted was a great boy. He called Cronin 'Sport,' which was a hell of a thing for a rookie. But the thing was, he was just as good as he thought he was. When he stepped up to hit, he was all business. You never saw such concentration in a hitter, young or old. He hit them as far as Foxx. That was all you had to know. He had that swing, you see."

Defense bored the young man. Cronin had to lasso him to get him out in the daisies to improve.

"All he wants to do is hit," the skipper lamented to Collins.

"Well," Eddie said, "if you could hit like that, wouldn't you?"

The club had Williams penciled in for one more year in the minors, to be spent with the Minneapolis club of the American Association. The twenty-year-old slugger gave Minneapolis fans a year to remember: a .366 batting average, 43 home runs, 142 RBIs. The Red Sox dispatched Chapman and his .340 batting average to Cleveland to make room. One temperamental outfielder moved to make way for another. But not quite the same. Chapman was testy, two-fisted, sharp-tongued. Ted?

"He gave me fits, sure," Cronin said. "Mostly about his fielding. But when he got mad it was usually at himself, because he was such a perfectionist. But no matter what, he always had that charm. You had to like him. And you had to admire him for what he was doing and for what he was trying to do."

Williams was the rare talent that lends stature to the game; he exuded an aura that transcended the game and enchanted all who watched him. The novelist David Markson said of Williams: "If you were lucky enough to be nine or ten years old when Williams came up, you had a talisman of power and splendor to carry with you for the rest of your life."

Williams came to the major leagues with immediate impact. There was never any doubt about him, and only one question: Just how good was he going to get?

The Yankees' veteran catcher Bill Dickey said of the new man, "I told people right from the beginning that he was going to get better and better."

The prediction must have intrigued people, since the young man was pretty good to start with—a .327 batting average, 31 home runs, and 145 RBIs, which is still the major-league record for a rookie.

Catcher Johnny Peacock (1937–44). Johnny batted .303 as a part-timer in 1938.

Williams was a marvelous addition, but the team again finished second, seventeen games behind the Yankees. Foxx joined with the rookie to give the Red Sox a most potent one-two punch, Jimmie batting .360 and leading with 35 homers. Doerr, Cronin, and Cramer all hit over .300, and the club added still another hard sticker in third baseman Jim Tabor, who batted .289 and drove in 95 runs. Tabor put on a personal fireworks display in the July 4 doubleheader against the Athletics in Philadelphia. (Holiday doubleheaders were traditional in those days.) In a Wild West show, baseball-style, the Sox bloodied Connie Mack's pitching in 17–7 and 18–12 wins (Boston pitching was none too sturdy either this July afternoon), with Tabor blasting three home runs in the opener—two of them grand slams—and another in the nightcap, for a total of 11 RBIs for the day. He was the first Red Sox player to hit three home runs in a game.

Right-hander Joe Heving (1938–40), whose brother Johnnie caught for the Red Sox in the late 1920s. A sharp relief pitcher, Joe's three-year Red Sox record was 31–11.

Pitching remained Boston's problem; only the thirty-nine-year-old Grove was effective, with a 15–4 record and a 2.54 ERA, which gave him the league lead in that telltale department for an all-time record ninth time (only two other pitchers have led as many as five times). Behind Lefty were three 11-game winners—Jack Wilson, lefty Fritz Ostermueller, and reliever Joe Heving. In contrast, the Yankees had seven pitchers winning in double figures.

If you look just above his right ankle, you'll see that Jimmie Foxx didn't hit everything over the fence.

The Yankees' four-year run of pennants came to an end in 1940, but it didn't help the Red Sox, who finished in a fourth-place tie with the White Sox, eight games behind pennant-winning Detroit. It was the closest they had come to the top since taking it all in 1918. The year's attendance of 716,234 set a new team record (which they would break in each of the next two years).

Outscoring everyone in the league except the Tigers, the Red Sox set a record by having each of their infielders hit more than twenty home runs: Foxx, 36; Doerr, 22; Cronin, 24; Tabor, 21. Foxx, Doerr, Cronin, and Williams each drove in more than 100 runs. Ted's batting average jumped to .344, third best in the league.

To their already lethal attack, the club added another .300 hitter, one with a familiar name—Dominic DiMaggio, who broke in at .301. Younger brother of Joe, Dominic lacked Joe's power but played with the same élan in center field (though in 1940 he was a right fielder).

The twenty-three-year-old Dominic was an alumnus of the same club that had sent his brother to the majors, the San Francisco Seals of the Pacific Coast League. Dominic might have been in the bigs a bit earlier except for a negative report from certain scouts, who said, "He only hits singles," as though this were some sort of failing. (By his career's end, in 1953, Dominic had a .298 lifetime average.)

Rookie left-hander Mickey Harris (1940–41, 1946–49) (*left*) with the veteran Lefty Grove.

(OPPOSITE PAGE) Joe DiMaggio (*left*) with his younger brother Dominic. (*Courtesy NBL*)

OSTON
HER

The club's heavy hitting was offset by the pitching staff's gruesome 4.89 ERA. Wilson was the only starter with a decent record (12–6). The forty-year-old Grove was down to 7–6 now and might have retired ("I was tired of trains and hotels and cities," Lefty groused), except that he was seven wins short of 300 and was determined to have them.

Boston's hard-hitting third baseman Jim Tabor (1938–44). (*Courtesy NBL*)

The 1941 season remains, for personal achievement, a landmark in baseball history. The pennant race in the American League was almost nonexistent, the Yankees winning over second-place Boston by seventeen games, clinching on the earliest date in major-league annals: September 4.

But the American League season was split into two enthralling parts that year. First was Joe DiMaggio's electrifying 56-game hitting streak, which was finally brought to a halt in Cleveland on the night of July 17. After that, attention gradually turned to what twenty-two-year-old Theodore Samuel Williams was up to. What he was up to was .400.

At the All-Star break, Williams was batting .405. And it was at this annual midseason, star-studded event that Williams cracked one of his most notable home runs. Coming to bat with his side down, 5–4, in the bottom of the ninth (the game was played in Detroit), Ted hit a two-out, three-run homer to win

Dom DiMaggio (1940–42, 1946–53) sliding safely into third in a June 1940 game at Fenway. Awaiting the throw is St. Louis Browns third baseman Harlond Clift.

Ted Williams in 1940.

the game, 7–5. It remains the most dramatic single blow in All-Star Game history, one that fed the pride of all New England.

It was on the last day of the season, however, that Williams put on a display of under-the-gun hitting that was to provide him with the glittering crown jewel of his career.

But before Williams made his bold and audacious rush at baseball's most stellar region, there was another historic event to be observed. It did not have the power and red-hot energy of youth but rather was the culminating moment of a long and distinguished career. It was the final stone in the formidable edifice that was the career of Robert Moses ("Lefty") Grove,

BOSTO

and it was put in place at Fenway on July 25. Working with all of his acquired guile and craft, the now forty-one-year-old one-time fireballer achieved the 300th and final victory of his career. Laboring through nine innings in 90-degree heat, Lefty outlasted the Indians, 10–6. Fittingly, it was his old Athletics teammate Jimmie Foxx who won it for him by banging a two-run triple in the last of the eighth that broke a 6–6 tie. The Sox scored two more runs, and Lefty nudged himself through the final inning to win it, calling the victory his "biggest thrill." Following Walter Johnson (416), Christy Mathewson (373), Grover Cleveland Alexander (373), and Eddie Plank (306), Lefty was just the fifth man to attain 300 wins in the twentieth century.

Dick Newsome (1941–43), Boston's surprise 19-game winner in 1941. (*Courtesy NBL*)

It was on the last day of the season that Ted Williams thrillingly demonstrated the grandeur and the isolation of greatness. Nursing his .400 batting average through the thinning days of September, Williams awoke on the morning of the season's final day with an average of .3995, or, as mathematically rounded off, .400. Baseball's magical kingdom.

Joe Dobson (1941–43, 1946–50, 1954).

The Red Sox had a doubleheader scheduled in Philadelphia, and Cronin offered to sit Ted down to insure that .400 average. But Williams, now all of twenty-three years old and brimming with the bravado and self-confidence that go with being twenty-three years old, insisted he would play. For Ted, one of the purest athletic bloods of all time, it was an opportunity to show the universe of baseball just what he was trying to prove—that he would become the greatest hitter of all time. To stand and defy the fates rather than take his .400 and pack it in was wonderfully audacious. And Williams more than met the challenge: In eight official at-bats on that chill, gray September afternoon, he delivered six hits, pushing his final average up to .406, making him baseball's last .400 hitter, proprietor of a digital peak that seems more and more remote with each passing season.

(Opposite page) Williams in batting practice.

Williams was the first .400 hitter since Bill Terry of the New York Giants checked in at .401 in 1930, and the first .400

American Leaguer since Harry Heilmann hit .403 in 1923. It was an all-around outstanding season for the Boston star; in addition to winning the first of his six batting titles, he led in home runs (37), runs (135), bases on balls (145), and slugging (.735—a figure bettered in baseball history by only Ruth, Gehrig, Foxx, and Rogers Hornsby). Nevertheless, the MVP Award went to DiMaggio.

Overshadowed by Williams was the 19–10 record turned in by right-hander Dick Newsome, who at the age of thirty-one was a rather well-seasoned rookie. The Sox also got a 12–5 year from right-hander Joe Dobson, who had been obtained over the winter from Cleveland, and introduced a young Texan who would soon be their ace—Cecil ("Tex") Hughson, a handsome righty with a fine assortment of pitches, who had a 5–3 record.

Pitcher Charlie Wagner (1939–42, 1946), whose flashy sartorial style earned him the nickname "Broadway." His best year was 1942, when he was 14–11.

An elated Ted Williams scoring after hitting the home run that won the 1941 All-Star Game for the American League. Greeting him are (No. 5) Joe DiMaggio and (No. 30) coach Merv Shea. Yankee second baseman Joe Gordon is in the background.

Lefty Grove and the ball with which he completed his 300th victory.

Johnny Pesky (1942, 1946–52). He hit over .300 six times for the Red Sox. (*Courtesy NBL*)

By the time the 1942 baseball season opened, the country had been at war for four months. Although a few stars, most notably Cleveland's Bob Feller and Detroit's Hank Greenberg, had entered military service, it would be another year before the big-league rosters began being depleted of regular players.

The 1942 Red Sox won more games than any Fenway club since the 1915 edition—93—but still finished in second place, nine games behind the Yankee steamroller. Boston's .276 batting average led the league for the fourth time in five years.

There were a few significant changes that year. On June 1, Jimmie Foxx was waived to the Chicago Cubs. His once awesome power now all but drained, Jimmie puttered around in the National League for several years with the Cubs and Phillies before retiring in 1945. A more positive change occurred at shortstop, where Cronin, now thirty-five years old, allowed himself to be moved aside for rookie Johnny Pesky, a trim twenty-two-year-old slap hitter who broke in with a .331 batting average and a league-high 205 hits. Cronin remained on the active roster as a part-timer until 1945.

A twenty-game winner in 1942 and again in 1946, Tex Hughson saw his career cut short by a bad arm.

On the mound, Boston had its first twenty-game winner since Wes Ferrell in 1935 when Hughson posted a 22–6 record. Tex also tied Bobo Newsom for the American League strikeout lead with 113, thus becoming the club's first whiff leader since Cy Young led the list way back in 1901, the team's first year of existence. (There would not be another Red Sox strikeout leader until Jim Lonborg in 1967, and then not another until Roger Clemens in 1988.)

For Williams, it was another year of pure thunder, as he followed his .400 season with a Triple Crown, leading the league in batting (.356), home runs (36), and RBIs (137). Again Ted was denied the MVP Award, which went to Yankee second baseman Joe Gordon, who had an excellent—though hardly great—season. It is probably the most flagrant example of wrong-headed voting in MVP Award history.

Soon after the close of the 1942 season, the reds and golds and oranges of the New England autumn dazzled the woods and fields from Maine to Connecticut, followed by the long meditations of winter. And when at last spring came, the snows had melted and the cycle of the seasons had turned the playgrounds green once again, it proved to be a baseball spring unlike others. It was as though the winter storms had carried off much that was familiar. When the Red Sox (and the same was true for every team) regrouped, some familiar faces were gone.

Williams was off to war, and so were Pesky, Dom DiMaggio, pitcher Charlie Wagner, and others, and more would follow. Baseball, under President Roosevelt's urging, struggled to keep going during the war.

Two-thirds of anybody's greatest outfield: Williams (*left*) and DiMaggio.

The 1943 Red Sox dropped to seventh place, as for the first time since 1927 the club was without a .300 hitter. Hughson's 12 victories led the staff. Cronin called back some memories by pinch-hitting 5 home runs, a new league record. Doerr set a new mark for second basemen by handling 349 straight chances over 54 games without an error. (He would top himself in 1948, with 414 chances over 73 games without an error.)

Manager Joe Cronin (*right*) giving a pat on the back to his successor at shortstop, Johnny Pesky.

(TOP LEFT)
Mike Ryba (1941–46). Primarily a relief pitcher, Mike pitched for the Sox right on through the war years. He was 12–7 in 1944, his top year.
(Courtesy NBL)

(TOP RIGHT)
After a successful career with Detroit, outfielder Pete Fox joined Boston in 1941 and played until 1945. He batted .315 in 1944.
(Courtesy NBL)

(BOTTOM LEFT)
Skeeter Newsome (1941–45). Skeeter, who was no relation to pitcher Dick Newsome, played the infield for Boston during the war years.

(BOTTOM RIGHT)
The White Sox' Luke Appling congratulating Bobby Doerr after Doerr's three-run homer helped win the 1943 All-Star Game for the American League. Check Appling's tie. It looks as though it was put together by the same people who designed the camel.

With so many players of varying caliber coming and going so rapidly in those years, a team's fortunes could change with stunning quickness—as did the Red Sox' in 1944, when Cronin and his men found themselves in the thick of a four-way pennant race with the Yankees, Browns, and Tigers. As late as September 3, the Sox were just one and a half games out of first place. But they had already seen Hughson and his 18–5 record and catcher Hal Wagner and his .332 batting average go off to service, and then they lost Doerr, who was batting .325. So it looked like a rugged September coming up—and it was indeed, an 8–16 September that dropped them to fourth place at the end, twelve games out. It was a season that the Red Sox must have been in a hurry to get over—on the final day they split a doubleheader with the White Sox that consumed just two hours and forty-eight minutes of playing time, Boston winning, 3–1, then losing, 4–1, with the second game being played in seventy minutes.

First baseman–outfielder George Metkovich (1943–46). They called George "Catfish" long before Jim Hunter appeared on the scene.

The vagaries of wartime ball saw the Red Sox return to seventh place in 1945. The only bit of interest for Bosox fans in this last of the wartime seasons was provided by rookie right-hander Dave ("Boo") Ferriss. Recently discharged from the military, the twenty-three-year-old Mississippian surprised and delighted the Fenway crowds by winning his first ten games, four of them shutouts. By pitching 22 straight scoreless innings from the start of his career, Ferris set an American League record that still stands. The big, likable pitcher finished the season with a 21–10 ledger; he was the first rookie to win twenty in the league since Wes Ferrell did it for Cleveland in 1929. Making Ferriss look even bigger on the Fenway mound was the fact that no other Red Sox pitcher won more than eight games that year.

Dave Ferriss (1945–50). In his first two years with the Red Sox, he was 46–16, then hurt his arm.
(Courtesy NBL)

The sight of young Ferriss winning so many games and the thought of all their stars returning now that the war was over were cause for Boston's eternally optimistic fans to look forward to the 1946 season.

Dave Ferriss studying a professional journal.

— 8 —

Success and Near-Success

For baseball, 1946 was a year of return and rejuvenation, and no team enjoyed it more than the Red Sox. Back from the scattered military camps and war zones were Ted Williams, Johnny Pesky, Bobby Doerr, Dom DiMaggio, Tex Hughson, Joe Dobson, and others. And it seemed they had all become bigger and stronger, for they led the team on a whirlwind journey through the schedule that delighted their long-suffering fans, who came out to Fenway in record numbers that summer—1,416,944, a record that would keep climbing over the next three years.

The Sox got off to a 21–4 start, which included a fifteen-game winning streak, still the longest in team history. The club was 11–3 in April and 21–6 in May (they began a twelve-game win streak on May 29) and continued playing solid ball until slowing to a 13–10 record in September, their poorest month of the season. They were an astounding 61–16 at Fenway, for a .792 winning percentage (a mark they repeated in 1949), which was one game under the 62-victory home record set by the 1932 Yankees.

"It was one of those things that occasionally happen in baseball," said Cronin, who managed his one and only pennant winner that year. "A team starts off hot, suddenly gets the idea it can't be stopped, and just keeps right on going."

Boston won 104 games and the pennant by a twelve-game margin over second-place Detroit. For a change, the club had some fine pitching to complement its hard-hitting attack. Second-year-man Ferriss bloomed to a 25–6 record, though the toughest pitcher was Hughson (20–11), leading the staff in ERA (2.75) and strikeouts (172). Ferriss won his first ten decisions, and later he and Hughson each had twelve-game winning streaks. Behind the aces were left-hander Mickey Harris (17–9), Joe Dobson (13–7), and some good bullpen work from lefty Earl Johnson and National League veteran Bob Klinger.

(Opposite page) Ted Williams. *(Courtesy NBL)*

(TOP LEFT)
Johnny Pesky.
(Courtesy NBL)

(TOP RIGHT)
Bobby Doerr.

(BOTTOM LEFT)
Joe Dobson.

(BOTTOM RIGHT)
Dom DiMaggio.
(Courtesy NBL)

At first base, the Sox had a one-year stopgap in veteran Rudy York, acquired from Detroit. One of the league's longtime solid hitters, York cracked 17 homers and drove in 119 runs. Doerr hit 18 homers and had 116 RBIs. Pesky batted .335 and picked up where he had left off in 1942—leading the league with 208 hits. Dom DiMaggio was a .316 hitter. And if there was any question about Ted Williams's batting eye after three years in service, the big left fielder dispelled it with 38 home runs, 123 RBIs, and a .342 batting average. Opposing pitchers walked him 156 times.

Fittingly, the All-Star Game was played at Fenway that year, and it was dominated by Williams, who had two homers and two singles in the American League's 12–0 runaway. In the bottom of the eighth, Ted and Pittsburgh right-hander Rip Sewell put on a vaudeville act of sorts when Sewell threw Ted one of his patented "blooper" pitches—a delivery that Rip arced about twenty-five feet into the air and parachuted over

(LEFT)
Joe Cronin pondering some decision or other.

(RIGHT)
Veteran first baseman Rudy York (1946–47), who in 1946 gave the Red Sox the last truly productive year of his career.

home plate. Williams timed it perfectly and, to the delight of everyone, Sewell included, blasted it into the right-field bleachers.

"The only man ever to hit a home run off the blooper," Sewell said of Williams.

Williams had by now achieved such stature as a hitter that the great game of baseball began to reshape itself in order to try and deal with him. At Fenway in mid-July, Cleveland manager Lou Boudreau devised and unveiled the "Williams shift." The maneuver was born out of frustration after Ted had devastated the Indians in the first game of a doubleheader with three home runs and eight runs batted in. In order to entice Ted to stop pulling and go to left field, Boudreau stacked his defense on the right side of the field—everyone except the third baseman, who was in the normal shortstop position, and the left fielder, who was in left-center. In devising this alignment (which only went into position when the bases were empty), Boudreau was willing to concede the single or double to left, should Williams decide to go that way.

Williams probably could have defeated the shift quickly and permanently by punching singles and doubles to left field, but that was not his style, either professionally or temperamentally. As other teams began using the maneuver against him, he did occasionally put one into left field—"A lot more than people realize," he said—but it meant tampering with his stance and his swing, and this he was reluctant to do. Also, he knew that his role was to hit the long ball and drive in runs; this was what he was paid to do, what the fans came to see. How many hits the shift cost him, how many points were trimmed from his lifetime average, will never be known—though, as Williams points out, he still won four batting titles after the shift was instituted and still ended up with a .344 lifetime average.

When he chose to, Williams could go the other way and defeat the shift, and he never did it more memorably than on September 13, against Boudreau and the Indians. Boston was

Four members of the 1946 Red Sox. *Left to right:* catcher Hal Wagner (1944, 1946–47), third baseman Rip Russell (1946–47), catcher Roy Partee (1943–44, 1946–47), and Pinky Higgins.

playing in Cleveland and needed one more win to clinch the pennant. In the first inning, Williams came to bat, watched the Indian defense go into their exaggerated overshift, then sliced a long fly ball to left-center. By the time left fielder Pat Seerey had run it down and thrown it in, Williams was around to score on the first and only inside-the-park home run of his career. Tex Hughson made it stand up in a 1–0 victory, and Boston had its first pennant since 1918.

Boston's opponents in the World Series were the St. Louis Cardinals, a collective epitome of "lean and hungry." Splendidly balanced, daring on the bases, underpaid (for many of them their World Series share was a near-equivalent of their year's salary), the Cardinals had won a grueling pennant race with the Brooklyn Dodgers, with whom they had ended the season in a dead heat and whom they then defeated in baseball's first pennant playoff. Manager Eddie Dyer's club was not known for power, but they did have batting champ Stan Musial (.365), the hustling Enos Slaughter, and sterling all-around

Wally Moses (1946–48). The veteran outfielder joined the Red Sox after a long, productive career with the Athletics and White Sox.

Ted Williams sliding home on the only inside-the-park home run of his career, against Cleveland in September 1946. It was the only run of the game in which the Red Sox clinched the 1946 pennant. Jim Hogan is the catcher, Bill Grieve the umpire.

defense, particularly in shortstop Marty Marion and center fielder Terry Moore. And most of all, they had a deep, gutty pitching staff, led by 21-game winning southpaw Howard Pollett. Virtually every man on the Cardinal team had come up through the club's minor-league system, and they played as one, with an élan rare on any ball club.

Tex Hughson (1942–44, 1946–49).

Boston won the Series opener in St. Louis, 3–2, on York's tenth-inning homer. The Cardinals evened it the next day as lefty Harry Brecheen pitched a 3–0 shutout.

In Fenway for Game 3, Ferriss put the Sox a game up with a 4–0 blanking, helped along by York's three-run homer in the first. The Cards battered Sox pitching for 20 hits and a 12–3 win the next day, tying the Series. Dobson then fired a four-hitter in Game 5, winning 6–3 and putting the Red Sox one game away from taking it all. The clubs then traveled by train for St. Louis.

Brecheen came back and tied the Series at three games apiece with a 4–1 victory, setting the stage for baseball's most glamorous occasion—the seventh game of the World Series—and fittingly, it was a most memorable game.

Ferriss started for Boston and right-hander Murry Dickson for St. Louis. The Cards broke a 1–1 tie with two runs in the bottom of the fifth, but Boston came back to tie it up in the top of the eighth. After pinch hitters Rip Russell and George Metkovich opened with a single and double, respectively, the Cardinals removed Dickson and brought in Brecheen, who had pitched a complete game victory the day before. Brecheen, known as "Harry the Cat" for his feline appearance, retired Wally Moses and Johnny Pesky without allowing a runner to advance. But then Dom DiMaggio doubled to right, scoring both runners and tying the game. In running out his hit, DiMaggio pulled a muscle and had to be replaced on the bases, and later in the outfield, by Leon Culberson. This soon proved to be significant.

Mickey Harris.

Dave Ferriss.

With Bob Klinger on the mound for Boston, Slaughter opened the bottom of the eighth with a single. The next two men were retired. With two out and Harry Walker at bat, Slaughter broke for second. Walker punched a soft liner into left-center. Culberson, playing in place of the sure-handed DiMaggio in center, handled the ball less than impeccably while the Slaughter Express went barreling nonstop around the bases, exhorted by more than 36,000 Cardinal fans, who were on their feet roaring to Enos to keep going. And keep going he did, running through the "stop" sign thrown up by third-base coach Mike Gonzalez, whipping around third, and burning up the final ninety feet to the plate as Culberson's relay went to Pesky. Doerr shouted to Pesky to go home with the ball, but the crowd noise drowned him out. Pesky hesitated for just an instant—long enough to earn himself a dubious niche in World Series annals—and then spotted Slaughter and fired the ball home. But it was too late, and probably would have been too late even had he not hesitated. Slaughter scored easily.

Dom DiMaggio forced at home during the 1946 World Series. The action occurred in the bottom of the first inning of Game 5. The catcher is Joe Garagiola, the umpire Lee Ballanfant.

The Cardinals are employing the shift against Williams at Sportsman's Park, St. Louis, during the 1946 World Series. There are three men on the right side of the infield, while center field is completely undefended.

The Red Sox threatened in the top of the ninth, but Brecheen prevailed and in relief earned his third victory of the Series.

For Williams, the only World Series he would ever play in was a great personal disappointment: just five singles and one run batted in. Ted received some balm a few weeks later when he was voted the league's Most Valuable Player, an award he probably should have won in 1941 and unquestionably in 1942.

The Red Sox were not to win another pennant until 1967, making the 1946 season an oasis in the club's historical landscape between 1918 and 1967.

The 1947 club played .500 ball for the season's first two months and never really got hot thereafter and were probably lucky to finish third. The problem was that the team's superb pitching staff was suddenly laid low by arm injuries to twenty-game winners Ferriss and Hughson, each of whom was slowed to a 12–11 record, and to Mickey Harris, who was just 5–4. Thus, three pitchers who in 1946 had been 62–26 fell in 1947 to 29–26. (Worse, none of the three ever fully recovered, and they ceased being factors on the Red Sox mound.) Dobson's 18–8 record was the best on the staff.

So Red Sox fans had to settle in 1947 for the glory of Ted Williams, who took his second Triple Crown with a .343 batting average, 32 home runs, and 114 RBIs, and probably would have done better had not wary American League pitchers walked him 162 times, second highest in history to Ruth's 170. (Despite the Triple Crown, Ted was again deprived of the MVP Award, losing by one vote to Joe DiMaggio, thanks to one mean-spirited, anti-Williams Boston writer named Mel Webb, who would not give Ted as much as a tenth-place vote. Webb had had an argument with Williams during the season.)

Pesky batted .324 and with 207 hits led the league for the third straight time, a record he shares with six other players in both leagues.

On June 13, 1947, night ball finally came to Fenway Park. Yawkey had been resisting the installation of arc lights for some

Loosening up.

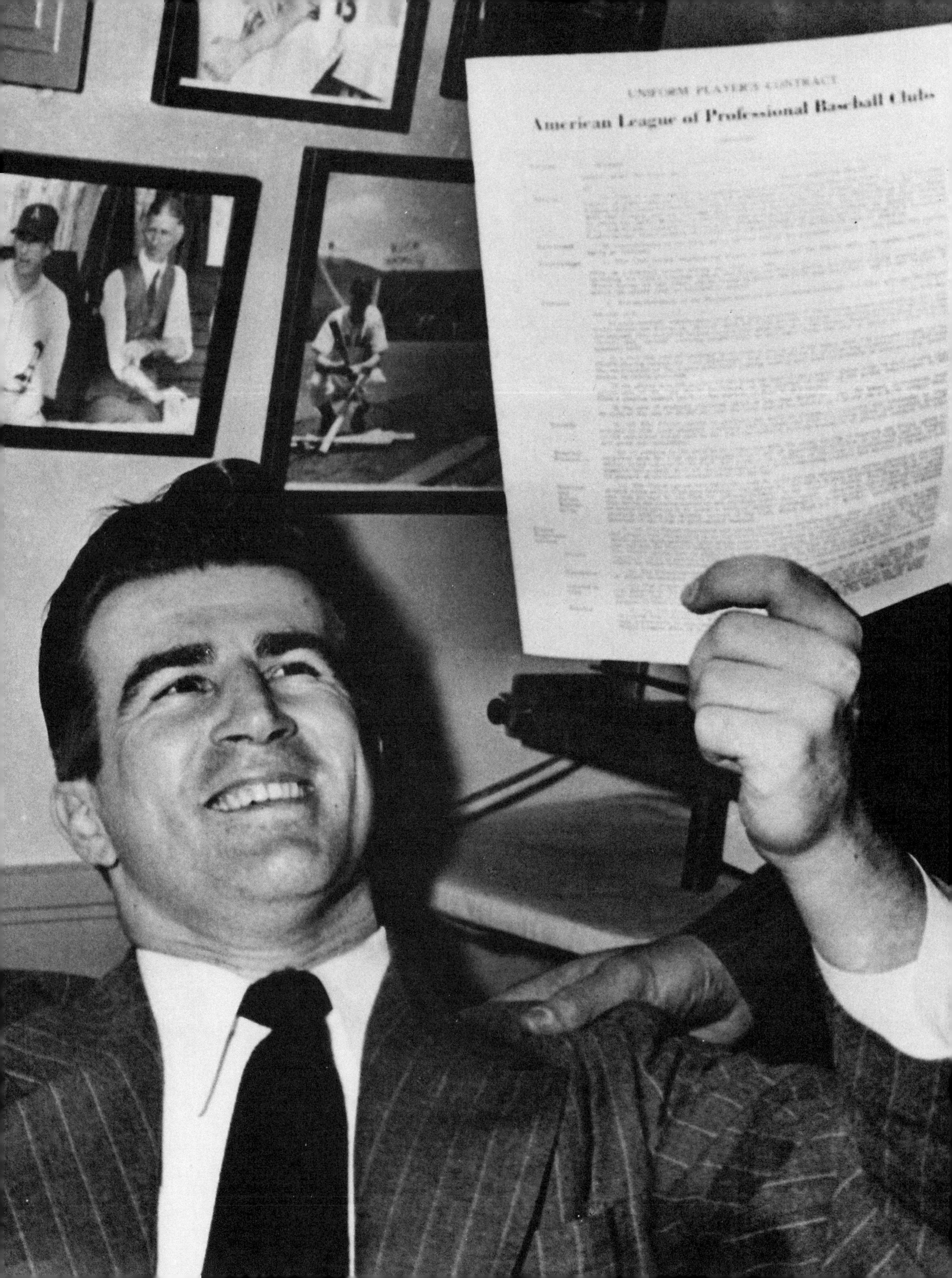
UNIFORM PLAYER'S CONTRACT
American League of Professional Baseball Clubs

(Opposite page) Johnny Pesky seems pleased with his 1947 contract.

time, but with thirteen of the other sixteen big-league clubs now equipped for night ball, the Red Sox owner bowed to the trend.

At the end of the season, the club made another move of some note. After thirteen years as manager, the now portly Joe Cronin relinquished the dugout and moved up to the front office as general manager, replacing the ailing Eddie Collins, who remained as consultant to Yawkey.

Cronin's first act as general manager was to sign Joe McCarthy as his successor. While managing the Yankees from 1932 to May 1946 (when he resigned because of ill health), during which time he won eight pennants and seven world championships, McCarthy had built a record as the game's most successful manager, impressing people with his baseball know-how and his ability to handle men. After nearly two full seasons away, Joe confessed that he had "been itching to get back into baseball." And get back into it he did, piloting the Red Sox through two of the most grueling and heartbreaking pennant races in club history.

The first big question for Joe, who was noted for his strict, businesslike approach, was: Would he be able to get along with that noted individualist, Theodore Williams? McCarthy answered the question immediately: "Any manager who can't get along with a .400 hitter should have his head examined." And, in fact, during McCarthy's two and a half years with the club, the two men developed a mutual respect that was deep and lasting. (McCarthy said that there was never any insubordination on Ted's part. "Of course," the skipper whimsically added, "I only gave him one order: Hit. He never disobeyed.")

In November 1947, the Red Sox swung a couple of deals with the St. Louis Browns, always a depressed ball club and always ready to make a deal, especially if there was cash involved. The cash involved this time amounted to $375,000, which went to St. Louis along with a small crowd of players in exchange for what was pretty much the pick of the Browns' roster—shortstop Vern Stephens and right-handers Jack Kramer and Ellis Kinder.

The deal was supposed to provide Boston with "pennant insurance." The acquisition of Stephens, a right-handed power hitter with a pronounced Fenway swing, made a third baseman of Pesky. In addition, the Sox added to the lineup the line-drive bat of Billy Goodman, a player of extraordinary versatility, who in 1948 played first base.

Sam Mele (1947–49, 1954–55). Sam broke in with a .302 average, highest of his career. (*Courtesy NBL*)

After a 14–23 April and May, the club was eleven and a half games out of first place. A 43–15 June and July turned that around. It became a tough, pounding, three-way race between Boston, New York, and Cleveland. At the end, Boston eliminated the Yankees and finished in a 96–58 tie with the Indians, necessitating a pennant playoff, which under American League rules was a single game.

Earl Johnson (1940–41, 1946–50), a left-handed reliever who gave the Sox some strong work in 1947 and 1948.

Boston won the coin flip, and the game was played at Fenway on October 4. The Indians sent to the mound left-hander Gene Bearden, a twenty-eight-year-old rookie who featured a knuckleball. Bearden had a fine 20–7 record in 1948, a showing he never came close to repeating. (His low-breaking, hard-to-hit knuckler was not a strike; the batters came to realize this, forcing him to pitch a bit higher, which he was unable to do effectively. But that was later.)

McCarthy had a strong array of starters—Dobson (16–10), Kramer (18–5), young left-hander Mel Parnell (15–8), and Kinder (10–7)—but the skipper had been working them hard down the stretch and didn't feel that any of them were strong enough to work the season's decisive game. So, in the most controversial decision of his career, he went to thirty-six-year-old right-hander Denny Galehouse, who was 8–8 that year.

"I didn't have anybody else," McCarthy explained. "My front-line starters were all used up. I could have started Parnell or Kinder or one of the others, but then I would have been second-guessed for starting a tired pitcher. No matter what you do," the philosophical McCarthy said, "you get second-guessed."

One Boston writer later published a story that suggested McCarthy pulled Galehouse out of the closet because none of the regular starters wanted the ball. The story was angrily refuted by Parnell, who called it "pure fiction, a terrible lie. Each of us would have given anything to pitch that game. . . . I felt McCarthy probably would pick Kramer. I never dreamed Galehouse. Neither did Denny. He was dumbfounded. He was shagging flies in the outfield during batting practice when McCarthy sent a clubhouse man for him. When Joe told him, Denny went white as a ghost. He took a short rest on the rubbing table and then went out to warm up."

One of the great hitting shortstops of all time, Vern Stephens (1948–52). In 1948, 1949, and 1950, he *averaged* 147 RBIs per year.

It probably would have made no difference whom the Red Sox started, for on that afternoon they were up against a force of almost maniacal determination in Boudreau. The Cleveland manager-shortstop, always a sterling performer under pressure, in that game made an art form of clutch hitting, blasting two home runs and two singles, as Bearden went on to a fairly easy 8–3 win, abetted by a big three-run homer by third baseman Ken Keltner.

Boston's 1948 outfield. *Left to right:* Sam Mele, Ted Williams, Stan Spence, Dom DiMaggio.

Adding to the city of Boston's disappointment was the fact that the Braves had won their first pennant since 1914; thus, the Red Sox' defeat deprived the city of what would have been its only all-Boston World Series. Red Sox fans had to settle for the glory of Ted Williams's fourth batting title, achieved with a .369 average.

Jack Kramer (1948–49). Ransomed from the Browns, Kramer gave the Red Sox a big 18–5 year in 1948, then faded out.

Three times the Red Sox and Yankees have decided the American League pennant on the final day of the season: 1904, 1949, and 1978. In 1904, Boston won on Jack Chesbro's famous wild pitch; in 1949 and 1978, the banner fell the other way.

For the second year in a row, the Red Sox started off slowly in 1949—5–6 in April, 15–10 in May, 15–15 in June. But then the club began to get hot: 18–12 in July, 24–8 in August, 19–5 in September—but 0–2 in October, and in those final two games lay the tale of the season.

Working the Yankee dugout for the first time that year was Casey Stengel, and the cagey old veteran of the baseball byways was never sharper as he manipulated and maneuvered an injury-ridden Yankee team that was outgunned by the Red Sox in almost every offensive department. Stengel had a quartet of high-grade starters in Vic Raschi, Allie Reynolds, Eddie Lopat, and Tommy Byrne and a red-hot reliever in Joe Page. Stengel also had Yogi Berra, Tommy Henrich, Hank Bauer, Phil Rizzuto, and, for part of the season, Joe DiMaggio.

The partial season began for DiMaggio at Fenway on June 28. After missing the club's first sixty-five games because of heel-spur surgery, Joe was inserted into the lineup for what was for him the equivalent of the first day of spring training. What he did to Red Sox pitching in that three-game series ranks just below his 56-game hitting streak in the DiMaggio book of legends. Joe hit four home runs, drove in nine runs, and led the Yankees to a memorable sweep.

Behind the bruising slugging of Williams and Stephens (they tied for the RBI lead, each with a mammoth 159), and the solid hitting of Pesky, Doerr, and Dom DiMaggio, the Sox

(LEFT)
Denny Galehouse (1939–40, 1947–49).

(RIGHT)
Joe McCarthy.

Employer and employee. Ted Williams and Tom Yawkey.

fought back into the race. In July and August, Dominic set a club record with a 34-game hitting streak, which brother Joe helped end with a shoe-top catch at Fenway on the night of August 9. In the face of Boston's hard-hitting attack, opposing pitchers issued the club 835 bases on balls, still the major-league record.

Stan Spence (1940–41, 1948–49). In between his tours with Boston, Spence had some fine years with Washington.

As far as Boston pitching was concerned, this was the year of Parnell and Kinder—Mel going 25–7 and Ellis 23–6. Behind them was Dobson, at 14–12.

The season finally boiled down to those two games in October with the Yankees. It was a schedule maker's dream—Boston coming into New York for a weekend finale with a one-game lead and two to play.

The Sox jumped off to a 4–0 lead in the Saturday afternoon game, but the Yankees worked their way back and, behind some brilliant relief by Page, won it, 5–4. The teams were now deadlocked, with one game to play.

On Sunday afternoon, a full house at Yankee Stadium watched Raschi and Kinder go at it. New York took a 1–0 lead in the bottom of the first, and the grim, fiercely competitive

Fenway Park in pregame repose.

Birdie Tebbetts (1947–50). The veteran catcher hit .310 for the Sox in 1950.

Billy Goodman (1947–57), the utility man who won a batting crown. (*Courtesy NBL*)

Raschi protected it inning after inning, matched by Kinder and his swooping curveballs. In the top of the eighth, McCarthy was forced to hit for Kinder. Boston did not score. Parnell took over in the last of the eighth, yielded a home run to Henrich and was gone. Hughson came in (it was his final big-league appearance) and loaded the bases. Jerry Coleman then hit a soft, sinking liner to right field that Al Zarilla dived for and missed by inches. The blow cleared the bases, giving New York a 5–0 lead.

A game Red Sox club scored three times in the top of the ninth, but Raschi, in whom Stengel showed great faith, hung on and completed his 5–3, pennant-clinching victory.

So it was two bitter, last-minute defeats in two years, with the second being the harder to swallow because all the Sox had needed was to win one of two at the end and because the team that beat them out was the Yankees.

Once more, all that Red Sox fans had to help them through the long New England winter were the exploits of Ted Williams, who led the league with 43 home runs (his career high), tied Stephens for the RBI lead, and lost the batting title—and a third Triple Crown—by two-tenths of a point to George Kell. Ted's high-flying year earned him his second MVP trophy.

The 1950 Red Sox tried to pound the league into submission with a year-long slugging assault and came near to succeeding. Led by batting champion Billy Goodman's .354, the club as a unit batted .302, the last major-league team to compile a .300 average. Pesky, Zarilla, DiMaggio, Williams, catcher Birdie Tebbetts, and rookie first baseman Walt Dropo batted over .300, while Stephens at .295 and Doerr at .294 were low men among the regulars. Goodman was a most unusual player. A versatile performer, at home anywhere in the infield or outfield, he had to hunt and peck to get into the lineup, but got into enough games and had enough at-bats to qualify for the batting title. Fortunately for the Sox, Billy was an easygoing man, with no ego problems.

(Top left)
Mel Parnell (1947–56). This superb left-hander was a twenty-game winner in 1949 and again in 1953.

(Top right)
Ellis Kinder (1948–55). The canny right-hander won 23 in 1949; in the early 1950s he became one of the league's top relievers, notching 27 saves in 1953.
(Courtesy NBL)

(Bottom left)
Walter Dropo (1949–52), who turned in a thunderous rookie year in 1950.
(Courtesy TV Sports Mailbag)

(Bottom right)
Outfielder Al Zarilla (1949–50, 1952–53), who batted .325 in 1950. He was part of the team that averaged .302, the last big-league team to bat over .300.
(Courtesy NBL)

"Whatever they wanted me to do was just fine with me," he said. "Nobody was ever better to me than Tom Yawkey and Joe McCarthy."

Stephens and Dropo tied for the RBI lead with 144 apiece. The 6-foot 5-inch Dropo broke in with one of the greatest rookie seasons ever—in addition to his 144 RBIs, he batted .322 and hit 34 home runs. He never came close to repeating his early success, however, and two years later was traded to Detroit.

Despite setting all-time club records for batting average and runs (1,027), the Sox finished third, four games behind the pennant-winning Yankees (whom they outscored by 113 runs) and one behind Detroit (whom they outscored by 190 runs). It simply was not an easy year in the American League, with the top four clubs each winning 92 or more games.

Dom DiMaggio led the league in stolen bases with a modest total of 15, which remains the lowest in major-league history for a leader in that department.

Boston suffered from falloff seasons by Parnell, who went from 25 wins to 18, and Kinder, who dropped from 23 to 14. The Sox still might have gone on to win if not for Ted Williams's injury in the All-Star Game, which in the past had been an occasion of celebration for Ted. But in the 1950 contest, played at Chicago's Comiskey Park, the Red Sox slugger shattered his left elbow crashing into the wall while making a fine running catch. The injury was serious enough to put Ted's career in jeopardy for a while. Though he was back by the end of the season, Williams claimed he was never the same hitter again.

Boston's hefty offense was displayed at Fenway on June 7 and 8 in a record-setting cannonading of the hapless St. Louis Browns. On June 7, the Sox smashed their way to a 20–4 victory, and the next day made that look tame by racking up a 29–4 drubbing, during which it was hard to tell when batting practice stopped and the game started. A multitude of big-league records were established during the two-day onslaught,

American League president Will Harridge presenting Billy Goodman with the silver bat emblematic of winning the batting crown in 1950. The presentation was made in May 1951.

A trio of Red Sox left-handers. *Left to right:* Chuck Stobbs (1947–51), Mel Parnell, and Mickey McDermott (1948–53).

Red Sox manager Steve O'Neill (*left*) and the man who would succeed him, Lou Boudreau. Boudreau wound up his playing career with the Red Sox in 1951–52, when he took over as skipper.

most notably a new one-game scoring high (29) and two-game marks for runs scored (49) and hits (51). In the 28-hit, 29–4 game, Doerr hit three home runs and Dropo and Williams each had two. An interesting sidebar to this game is that McCarthy made no substitutions, playing his nine starters all the way through, even though the Sox were up by 22–3 after five innings.

Despite all this resonant and voluminous hitting, the club had gotten off to a sluggish start, barely playing .500 ball after its first sixty-two games. It was at this point that a tired and weary Joe McCarthy resigned and retired from baseball, this time permanently.

"I guess it begins to catch up to you," Joe said later. "I began to feel I wasn't a good manager anymore. So I quit."

As he had in New York, McCarthy left behind a legacy of admiring ballplayers. Williams said of him, "Joe McCarthy got more out of his players than anybody. He was the complete manager." Pesky had high praise for Cronin but maintained, "Joe McCarthy was the best."

Despite the esteem in which he was held by his players, it was McCarthy's successor, Steve O'Neill, who came in and put the team on the roll that almost brought them a pennant. After going 32–30 under McCarthy, the Sox played at a torrid 62–30 pace under his replacement, including a blistering 24–6 in August. But in the end they fell four games short.

"In 1948, 1949, and 1950," Billy Goodman lamented, "we missed winning three pennants by a grand total of six games. That was pretty rough."

— 9 —

Quiet Years

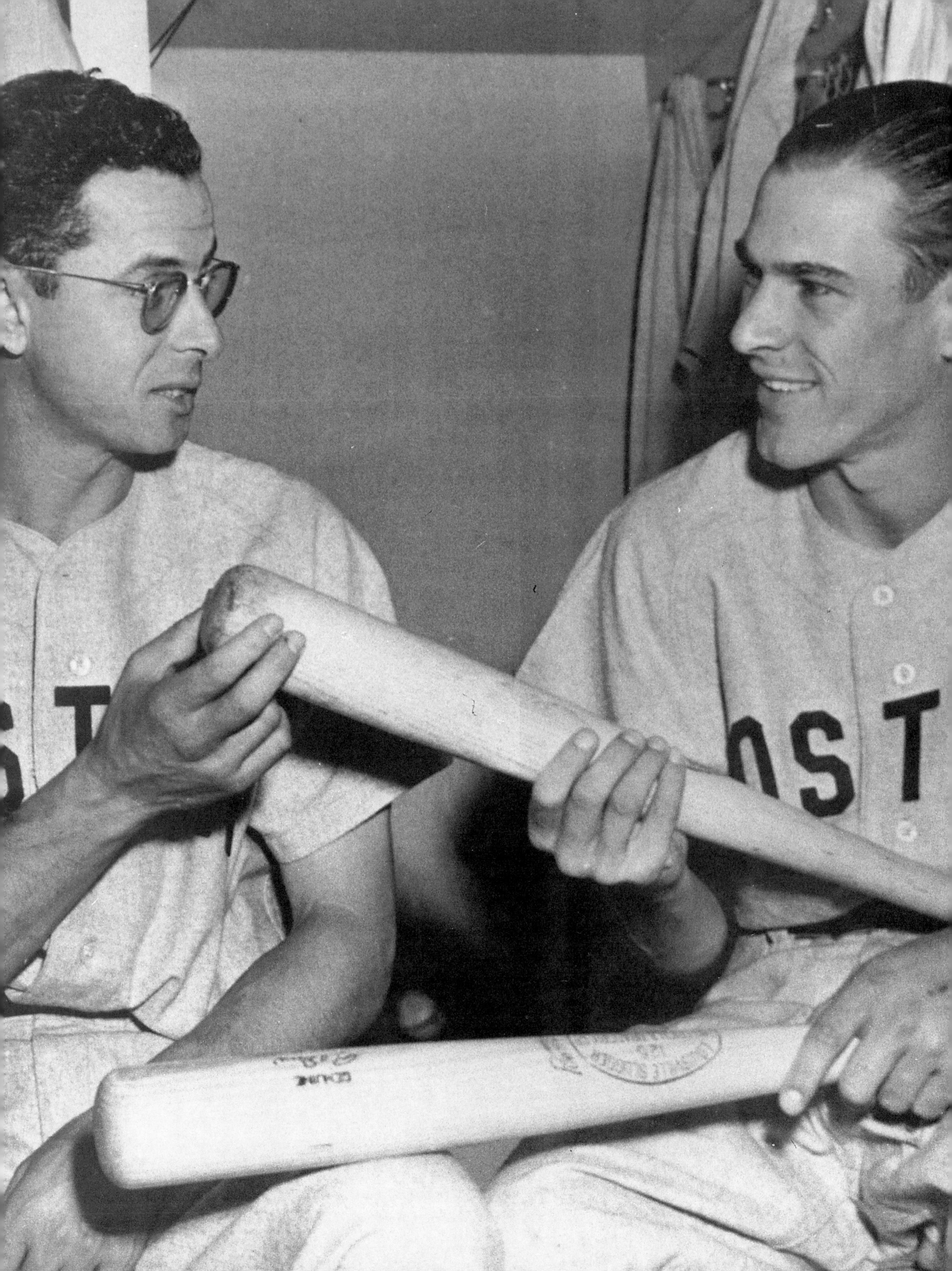
ST
OST

The Red Sox had won more than ninety games three years in a row and had nothing to show for it. With that effort, they had achieved a peak they were unable to go beyond. They finished third again in 1951, under O'Neill, but were never a factor in the pennant race. This was a Yankee decade: Casey Stengel's club would take every pennant in the 1950s except in 1954 and 1959.

The 1951 season is remembered by Red Sox fans primarily for the exploits of Clyde Vollmer in the month of July. A journeyman outfielder who batted .251 for the season, Vollmer tore up the pasture for one month with a dazzling display of hitting. From July 4 through July 31, he hit 13 home runs and drove in 40 runs. His hits—many of them in the clutch—included two grand slams, and on July 26 he hit three homers in a game. When the month was over, he ceased being Babe Ruth and went back to being Clyde Vollmer.

For Boston, the near-miss disappointments of 1948 and 1949 became more and more poignant to contemplate as the club began an annual journey to nowhere that reminded some of the older fans of the pre-Yawkey years. The Red Sox teams in the 1950s and 1960s weren't as bad as the last-place perennials of the 1920s—there were third-place finishes in 1957 and 1958—but the years from 1952 to 1966 are an arid passage in Boston baseball history.

The team that had batted .302 in 1950 did not remain intact for long. A chronically ailing back brought the career of Bobby Doerr to a premature end after the 1951 season. The greatest second baseman in Red Sox history was just thirty-three years old. In 1952, Pesky and Dropo went to Detroit in a multiplayer deal that brought third baseman George Kell, among others, to Boston. And in 1952, after playing just a handful of games, Williams was activated by the Marines and eventually went to Korea. Following an emotion-filled "Ted Williams Day" ceremony on April 30, 1952, the thirty-three-year-old living legend

(OPPOSITE PAGE)
Dom DiMaggio (*left*) and Billy Goodman in 1951.

played and won the game with a seventh-inning home run, then went off to war for the second time, not to return until August 1953.

Clyde Vollmer (1950–53): one blazing month in 1951.

Lou Boudreau, who had joined the Sox in 1951 after being released by Cleveland, took over as manager in 1952 and remained for three years. The farm system was turning out some good young players who began being filtered into the lineup; they included pitchers Mickey McDermott, Willard Nixon, and Ike Delock, first baseman Dick Gernert, catcher Sammy White, and outfielder Jimmy Piersall.

McDermott and Piersall were vivid personalities. Mickey seemed almost a parody of the stereotypical "flaky" left-hander, possessing in equal parts eccentricity, charm, and naiveté, and, most important, an explosive fastball. Piersall was a rare bird of dazzling plumage. Jimmy could play, to the extent that Casey Stengel once stated that he had never seen a better outfielder.

Piersall could be an ingratiating man, intelligent and witty. But there was also an antic, unstable side to him that irritated many players, teammates and opponents alike. There were a couple of highly publicized fistfights with the Yankees' Billy Martin and with McDermott.

That's Ted Williams scoring before Yogi Berra can tag him.

Piersall was sometimes very amusing, but at other times his behavior made people wonder and frown. One night at Fenway, with the veteran Satchel Paige on the mound, Piersall was on first base and began flapping his arms and yelling, "Oink, oink, oink." Paige, who had been around a long time and thought he had seen everything, was unnerved. He stepped off the mound and stared curiously at the young man who was taunting him. Piersall continued yelling at Paige. Clearly annoyed, Paige went on to load the bases and then feed a game-winning grand slam to Sammy White.

Ray Scarborough (1951–52). Ray was 12–9 in 1951, his only full year in Boston.

Boston fans may have been amused by Piersall, but what they were seeing was a young man in torment. After the game, St. Louis catcher Clint Courtney said, "I believe that man is plumb crazy." Courtney's unadorned analysis was recalled a month later when Piersall had a breakdown and entered a sanitarium. (His story was later told in his autobiography, *Fear Strikes Out,* and also in the movie of the same name.) Jimmy returned the following season, 1953, and resumed his career, playing until 1967, less volatile but still spirited and uninhibited: when he hit his 100th big-league home run, while playing with the Mets in 1963, he celebrated the occasion by running backwards around the bases.

There were a few things to remember about the 1953 season, the first occurring at Fenway on June 18. Just a few years after the Red Sox had set an all-time one-game scoring high, they wrote another gaudy line into the books by staging a seventeen-run inning. This prodigious outburst came in the seventh inning of a game against the Tigers. The Sox sent twenty-three batters to the plate, twenty of whom reached base, fourteen by hits, six by walks. Twenty-year-old outfielder Gene Stephens put himself into the record books by cracking three hits during the orgy, two singles and a double. No other player in the twentieth century has ever had three hits in an inning. (Not too many have had three at-bats in an inning.)

Ted Williams: back to the wars in 1952.

(TOP LEFT)
Lou Boudreau, Red Sox manager from 1952 to 1954.

(TOP RIGHT)
One of the great third baseman of all time, George Kell was acquired from the Tigers in June 1952 and played with the Red Sox until early in 1954. He batted .307 in 1953.

(BOTTOM LEFT)
Jimmy Piersall (1950, 1952–58). Casey Stengel said he never saw a better defensive outfielder.

(BOTTOM RIGHT)
A power-hitting first baseman, Dick Gernert played for Boston from 1952 through 1959.
(Courtesy NBL)

The sweetest memory of the season for Red Sox fans was the return of Ted Williams. The great slugger was weary and worn out; he had flown thirty-nine missions in Korea, including one in which his jet was struck by enemy ground fire, forcing him to bring in a plane that was billowing smoke and streaming thirty feet of flames. When he returned late in the season, he wasn't sure he wanted to play. But the Red Sox and various league officials talked him into it. So he limbered up with some batting practice, pinch-hit a home run in his first at-bat in Fenway, and went on to get into 37 games, hit 13 home runs, and bat .407.

After the 1953 season, the Red Sox engineered one of their better trades when in exchange for McDermott and outfielder Tom Umphlett they acquired outfielder Jackie Jensen from the Washington Senators. Jensen was the onetime "Golden Boy" from the University of California, where he had been an All-American football player as well as baseball star. The Yankees had signed him for a considerable bonus, intending to groom

A quartet of Red Sox players posing at Yankee Stadium in 1952. *Left to right:* outfielder Faye Throneberry (1952, 1955–57), infielder Ted Lepico (1952–59), Jimmy Piersall, and pitcher Bill Henry (1952–55). *(Courtesy NBL)*

Red Sox shortstop Milt Bolling making a vain effort to flag one up the middle. Milt played for Boston from 1952–57. (This picture dates from 1953. Note that players still left their gloves on the field between innings.)

him as Joe DiMaggio's successor. The unexpected rise of Mickey Mantle, however, had made Jensen expendable, and the Yankees dealt him to Washington.

Strong right-handed-hitting batters were always attractive to the Red Sox, and in order to land Jensen they had to trade away McDermott, who had been 18–10 that year and seemed to be coming into his prime. At the age of twenty-five, however, Mickey had hit his peak and was never an effective pitcher again. Jensen went on to a solid and productive career at Fenway, driving in more than 100 runs five times and leading the league three times. In 1958, he was voted the American League's Most Valuable Player, having put together a summer of substantial slugging, hitting 35 home runs and driving in 122 runs. After leading in RBIs for the third time in 1959, the thirty-two-year-old Jensen stunned everyone by giving in to a lifelong fear of flying and announcing his retirement. He came back two years later, put in a mediocre season and then quit again, this time for good.

Sammy White (1951–59), one of the outstanding catchers in Red Sox history.
(Courtesy NBL)

(Top left)
Mel Parnell.
(Courtesy NBL)

(Top right)
Mickey McDermott, a left-hander in the classic mold: fast, wild, colorful, unpredictable.

(Bottom left)
Bill Henry, who started and relieved for the Red Sox.
(Courtesy NBL)

(Bottom right)
Harry Agganis.
(Courtesy NBL)

Jimmy Piersall.
(*Courtesy NBL*)

Jackie Jensen (1954–59, 1961).
(*Courtesy NBL*)

In 1954, Ted Williams was looking forward to his first full season since 1951. At the age of thirty-five, baseball's number-one hitter had already lost the greater part of five full seasons to military service, and he was determined to make the best of the few years of playing time he had left. On March 1, however, the first day of spring training, a frisky Williams hustled after a sinking line drive in batting practice, lost his footing, stumbled, and fell and broke his collarbone. He was out of the lineup until May 16. When he finally made his 1954 debut on that day, in a doubleheader at Detroit, he drove out eight hits in nine at-bats, without benefit of spring training.

"What does this tell you about spring training?" a Boston newspaperman asked Cronin.

"It tells me that there's only one Ted Williams," the GM said.

This was the year the Red Sox started twenty-four-year-old Harry Agganis at first base. Agganis was already a New England star, even before accepting a $40,000 bonus to draw on a Red Sox uniform, having been an All-American quarterback at Boston University and the number-one draft choice of the Cleveland Browns, who saw him as successor to the estimable Otto Graham. But Harry opted for baseball, and he wanted to play it in Fenway, which he had already sold out while quarterbacking BU.

After a season in Triple-A with Boston's top farm club at Louisville, Agganis took over first base at Fenway in 1954. His .251 batting average disappointed him, and he vowed to do better. After twenty-five games in 1955, he was batting .313. In late May, a bout with pneumonia hospitalized him for ten days. Anxious to play, he returned to the lineup prematurely (in the opinion of some doctors) and within a few days was suffering from fever and chest pains and was hospitalized again, with a severe pulmonary infection that was complicated by phlebitis (the inflammation of a vein).

Opposing pitchers got whiplash just from watching.
(*Courtesy NBL*)

On June 27, Agganis suddenly died of what the doctors at Cambridge's Sancta Maria Hospital described as a "massive pulmonary embolism," or in lay terms, a blood clot. The "Golden Greek" was just two months past his twenty-fifth birthday.

These were the years when Williams lost two batting championships that should have been his. Under then existing rules, a player had to have a minimum of 400 official at-bats to qualify for the title. In 1954, Ted's .345 average was the best, but his 386 at-bats left him short of qualifying. In 1955, his .356 was easily the highest, but again his 320 at-bats disqualified him. When it was noted that he always received a large number of walks—136 in 1954, 91 in 1955—and that denying him these titles was an injustice, a rules change was put into effect that made plate appearances rather than official at-bats the determining factor in deciding a batting champion.

Leo Kiely (1951, 1954–56, 1958–59). He came up as a starter for Boston, then was converted to a reliever.

Smiling for the photographer. *Left to right:* Ted Lepico, Eddie Joost (1955), Billy Goodman, and Norm Zauchin (1951, 1955–57). A big first baseman, Zauchin hit 27 homers in 1955, his only full year with the team.

Boudreau was fired as manager after the 1954 season and was replaced by the club's former third baseman Pinky Higgins, whom Yawkey and Cronin had been grooming for the job. Pinky ran the club for four full years, always doing better than .500 but never finishing higher than fourth.

It looks as though manager Pinky Higgins is pondering a tough decision.

On July 14, 1956, Mel Parnell no-hit the White Sox at Fenway, 4–0. It was the first no-hitter thrown by a Red Sox pitcher since Howard Ehmke's in 1923. For the thirty-four-year-old left-hander, it was a most gratifying moment—he had been struggling with arm miseries for three years. Soon after, however, he tore a muscle in his left elbow, and his career was over. Parnell's 123 lifetime victories remain the most by a Red Sox left-hander.

Ever determined to bring a pennant to Boston no matter what the cost, Yawkey in the spring of 1957 stunned the universe of baseball by making a flat-out offer to Cleveland of $1 million for their hard-throwing young left-hander Herb Score, who in just two years had dazzled the league with his prowess. This was by far the largest cash sum ever offered for a ball-

An aerial view of Fenway Park.
(*Courtesy NBL*)

(Top left)
Outfielder Gene Stephens (1952–53, 1955–60). Always a part-time player, Stephens batted .293 in 1955.

(Top right)
Right-hander Frank Sullivan (1953–60). He was 18–13 in 1955, leading the league in victories.

(Bottom left)
Haywood Sullivan (1955, 1957, 1959–60), who went from rookie catcher to club owner.

(Bottom right)
Mickey Vernon (*left*) and Ted Williams in 1956. Vernon, who played for Boston in 1956–57, was a longtime American League first baseman and two-time batting champion. He hit .310 in 1956.

player. Cleveland general manager Hank Greenberg was admittedly tempted but had to turn it down, saying that Score was "going to become one of the greatest southpaws in history." And he no doubt would have; but shortly after the season opened, Score was hit in the eye by a line drive struck by the Yankees' Gil McDougald and was never the same pitcher again.

That was the year that the always remarkable Ted Williams became even more so. At the age of thirty-nine, Williams built his high tower to an even greater elevation with a .388 batting average, baseball's most ethereal since his own .406 in 1941. If

Willard Nixon (*left*) and Jackie Jensen celebrating a victory over the Yankees in August 1956. Nixon (1950–58) started and relieved for Boston. The right-hander's best year was 1955, when he was 12–10.

the season had lasted a bit longer, there is no telling to what heights he might have gone, since he batted .453 over the second half of the season and better than .650 the last ten days. His .388 (which buried Mickey Mantle's .365) made him the oldest batting champion. This impressive record lasted only long enough for him to become a year older, as he won the title again in 1958 at the age of forty, this time with a more modest .328, edging out teammate Pete Runnels, who finished at .322. (Runnels took the title in 1960, with a .320 average, and again in 1962, with a .326 average.)

Tom Brewer (1954–61). He was 19–9 in 1956, his top year.

The Sox now had Frank Malzone at third base. A product of their farm system, Malzone over the years established himself as Boston's best all-around third baseman since the World War I days of Larry Gardner. With Malzone, Jensen, Runnels, Piersall, and Williams, and Sammy White catching, the Red Sox had the makings of an outstanding club, except for suffering once again from a shortage of quality pitching. Right-handers Tom Brewer, Ike Delock, Willard Nixon, and Frank Sullivan won a modest amount of games during these years, but never enough.

Higgins left midway through the 1959 season, replaced by Billy Jurges, who had been an outstanding shortstop in the National League in the 1930s. The year also saw Cronin elected president of the American League, completing a Horatio Alger story, baseball-style. The son of Irish immigrants had risen from the sandlots of San Francisco to player, player-manager, general manager, Hall of Famer, and finally league president. Cronin was replaced as Boston's GM by, ironically, the man he had replaced as Red Sox manager in 1934, Bucky Harris. (Baseball's old-boy network was still in hearty operation.)

In 1959, there was also the elevation to the Red Sox of infielder Elijah ("Pumpsie") Green, who would today be barely noticeable in big-league annals if not for the fact that he was Boston's first black player. (The switch-hitting Pumpsie had a .246 lifetime average.) That it took the Red Sox twelve years

(LEFT)
Ike Delock (*left*) and Jimmy Piersall. Delock (1952–53, 1955–63) had his best year in 1958, going 14–8. Like fellow right-handers Nixon and Brewer, Ike was a product of Boston's farm system.

(RIGHT)
Frank Malzone (1955–65), one of the outstanding third basemen in Red Sox history.

Ted Williams (*right*) signing another contract. General manager Joe Cronin is seated at the left, manager Pinky Higgins is standing behind them.

(TOP LEFT)
Ted Williams in 1958.

(TOP RIGHT)
Billy Jurges, Red Sox manager in 1959–60.

(BOTTOM LEFT)
Gary Geiger, Red Sox outfielder from 1959 to 1965. He batted .302 in 1960, his best season.

(BOTTOM RIGHT)
Vic Wertz (1959–61). This veteran American League long-baller played first base for Boston. In 1960, he knocked in 103 runs.

after the pioneering season of Brooklyn's Jackie Robinson in 1947 to integrate their roster was a source of dismay to many Boston fans. The club's tardy start in the acquisition of black talent was no doubt costly, with such high-grade players as Willie Mays, Frank Robinson, Roberto Clemente, Ernie Banks, Elston Howard, and Hank Aaron having gone to other teams.

The Ted Williams era in Boston officially came to an end on the chill, gray afternoon of September 26, 1960. He had labored through a .254 season in 1959 (that uncharacteristic average was due to a neck injury that hampered him at bat) but had refused to retire on that note, even though Yawkey hinted that it might be time. Ted knew he was better than .254 and set out to prove it.

Williams's 1960 season was an excellent one by any standard; for a forty-two-year-old, it was exceptional. He batted .316 and hit 29 home runs in 310 at-bats. And to a career of many moments, he added the crowning one in his final time at bat.

In this, his last big-league game, Williams had been trying to hit one out. After having just missed putting one in the seats in his previous at-bat, he came to the plate for the last time in the eighth inning. (Even though Boston was going to wrap up the season with a weekend series in New York, Ted had resolved to observe his last good-byes at Fenway.) On the mound was Baltimore Oriole right-hander Jack Fisher, born in 1939, Ted's rookie year. After running the count to 1–1, Fisher delivered a fastball that was just a bit fatter than he wanted, and Ted's bat snapped at it. Here was the raw meat he had been feeding on for the last two decades; it had never got away before and it wouldn't now. Ted hit it soaring through the gray, soggy air and out into the Red Sox bullpen, for his 521st and final big-league home run, saying farewell as no slugger ever had, or has since.

"They reacted like nothing I have ever heard," Williams said of the crowd. "They cheered like hell, and as I came around the cheering grew louder and louder." He thought about tipping

Williams in 1959, one year from retirement. (*Courtesy NBL*)

A high-level discussion on the art of hitting is taking place in the Boston clubhouse. *Left to right:* Jackie Jensen, Frank Malzone, and Pete Runnels.

his cap (something he had always declined to do). "But by the time I got to second base I knew I couldn't do it. It just wouldn't have been me."

Nor is it likely the fans would have wanted him to be anyone but himself. He had brought more pride and glory to the Red Sox than any player in the club's history, and he had always done it his way. The boy from San Diego—geographically, as far away as you could get—had become as New England as any of them: proud, independent, ruggedly taciturn when he chose to be; an artisan who worked his craft to a high sheen of personal satisfaction, a man who valued his privacy, who cherished simple values. And the last man to bat .400.

(LEFT)
Pumpsie Green (1959–62), Boston's first black player.

(RIGHT)
Boston's tireless relief ace, Mike Fornieles (1957–63).

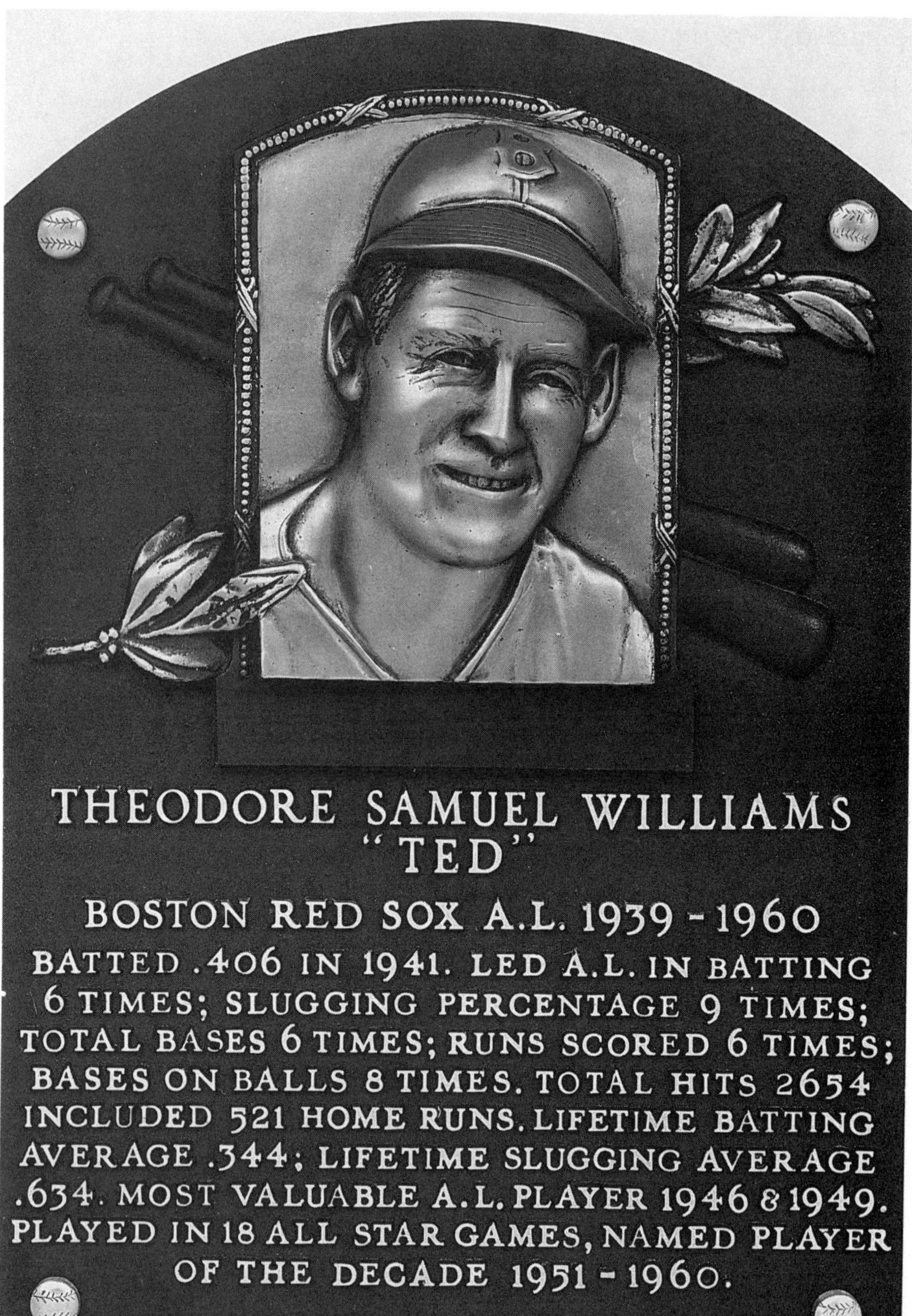

The Ted Williams plaque in Cooperstown. (*Courtesy NBL*)

— 10 —

"The Impossible Dream"

The laws of probability say it can't be done, but the Red Sox did it anyway. Just as the Yankees had a Mantle waiting when DiMaggio retired, so Boston, as unlikely as it sounds, had a replacement waiting to go to left field. Carl Yastrzemski wasn't quite a Williams, but for twenty-three years the Red Sox were more than satisfied, and so was everyone else who watched this eminently gifted, all-around player at work. What began in the spring of 1961 in Fenway Park's left field was to culminate in January 1989, with Yastrzemski's election to the Hall of Fame.

A product of eastern Long Island, Yastrzemski was a sophomore at Notre Dame, where his fierce, fluid left-handed power swing had attracted a $40,000 bonus offer from the Yankees. The young man's father, however, placed a much higher value on his son's abilities—$100,000. Boston scouts went out to Knute Rockne's old campus, made their evaluation, and agreed. Tom Yawkey backed them up.

Yastrzemski played his first year of pro ball (he was a second baseman then) with Raleigh in the Carolina League, where he banged the ball for a .377 average. The following year, 1960, he was with Minneapolis of the American Association (the same club Williams used as his springboard to the majors), where a .339 average told his employers he was ready.

It wasn't easy breaking in as "Ted Williams's replacement," and Yaz did it modestly, batting .266. One man who never doubted the youngster would do better was Williams himself. Ted admired Yaz's intensity and desire at home plate. "He positively *quivered* waiting for that next pitch," Williams said.

With experience, plus some fine-tuning from Williams, Yastrzemski came along quickly: .296 in his second year, and then a batting title (.321) in his third year, 1963.

It was Yastrzemski's misfortune to arrive at Fenway at a particularly dismal time in Red Sox history—the club's most arid spell, in fact, since the 1920s. During his first six years in

(OPPOSITE PAGE)
The new man in left field, Carl Yastrzemski (1961–83).

Boston, the club finished sixth, eighth, seventh, eighth, ninth, and ninth. Managers came and went—Jurges had been fired during the 1960 season, and Higgins came back; Pinky was replaced by Johnny Pesky in 1963; and in 1965, the skipper was former National League second baseman Billy Herman.

In 1961, the Sox had the American League Rookie of the Year in right-hander Don Schwall, who broke in with a 15–7 record. A year later, however, he was 9–15 and was traded to Pittsburgh. In 1962, there were some more individual achievements to stir fan interest: Pete Runnels took the batting championship (.326) and right-handers Bill Monbouquette and Earl Wilson each pitched no-hitters, Wilson's at Fenway on June 26 over the Angels, 2–0, and Monbouquette's on August 1 over the White Sox, 1–0 (defeating Early Wynn, who was in quest of his 298th big-league victory). A second-inning walk to Al Smith deprived "Mombo" of a perfect game.

Pete Runnels (1958–62), a man with an educated bat. He took batting titles in 1960 and 1962 and batted over .300 five straight times for Boston.

Don Buddin (*left*) and Chuck Schilling. Buddin (1956, 1958–61) was Boston's regular shortstop for five years, while Schilling (1961–65) was a slick glove at second base.

Monbouquette was the ace during these lean years. On May 12, 1961, he set a new club record by fanning seventeen Washington Senators, breaking the mark of fifteen set by Smoky Joe Wood in 1911. In 1963, Monbouquette was 20–10 for a seventh-place club.

Jim Pagliaroni (1955, 1960–62), a big, right-handed-hitting catcher.

The Red Sox had the league RBI leader in 1963 in first baseman Dick Stuart, a big right-handed powerhouse who had 118 RBIs and also hit 42 home runs. But no matter what he accomplished with the bat—and it was plenty—Stuart will always be remembered for his fielding, or for what resembled fielding. They called him "Dr. Strangeglove," and they said he led the league in waving at ground balls. Once, when he handled three ground balls cleanly in one inning, each time flipping perfectly to the pitcher covering, he got a standing ovation from his teammates when he returned to the dugout. Stuart, according to his manager Johnny Pesky, was a natural-born designated hitter who had come to the majors ten years ahead of his time. In 1964, Stuart hit 33 homers and drove in 114 runs, but after leading first basemen in errors for the second year in a row, it was felt he was allowing more runs than he was driving in, and he was traded to the Philadelphia Phillies.

Boston's Rookie of the Year pitcher in 1961, Don Schwall (1961–62).

For a few years in the early 1960s, Fenway fans delighted in watching a huge right-handed relief pitcher come walking in from the bullpen to ice a Red Sox victory. His name was Dick Radatz, he towered at six feet six inches and some 230 pounds (his nickname was "The Monster"), and from 1962 to 1964 he was as good a relief pitcher as ever lived. He was a one-pitch man, but that pitch was a blur of a fastball.

During his three great years, Radatz was 40–21, with 78 saves; he worked 414 innings, yielded just 292 hits, and had 487 strikeouts. In 1964, he appeared in 79 games, which at the time was the major-league record. It may have been too many: He lost an edge after that and in 1966 was traded to Cleveland.

Boston's two-sport man, Gene Conley (1961–63). The six-foot eight-inch pitcher also played for the Boston Celtics.

In 1964, the Red Sox introduced into their lineup a nineteen-year-old outfielder with a Fenway swing, Tony Conigliaro. A native of nearby Swampscott, Conigliaro busted

That's Boston's Eddie Bressoud (1962–65) desperately reaching for home plate. Umpire Joe Paparella ruled that Yankee catcher Elston Howard made the tag in time.

(LEFT)
Bill Monbouquette (1958–65), Boston's ace pitcher in the early 1960s. He was 20–10 in 1963, the team's only twenty-game winner between 1954 and 1967.

(RIGHT)
Russ Nixon (1960–65, 1968), Red Sox catcher. He played in the big leagues for twelve years and never stole a base.

Right-hander Earl Wilson (1959–60, 1962–66) kissing the ball with which he completed his no-hitter over the Angels at Fenway on June 26, 1962. With him is catcher Bob Tillman (1962–67).

"The Monster" in action: Dick Radatz nailing down another one.

24 homers and batted .290 in his rookie year. He was held to 111 games because of injuries—a dark omen for what was destined to be a tragically short career.

On September 16, 1965, right-hander Dave Morehead pitched the game of his life when he no-hit Cleveland, 2–0, at Fenway. It was the fourteenth no-hitter in Red Sox history and the fourth in ten years. For the twenty-two-year-old Morehead, who was 10–18 that year, it was the capstone of a career that began to unravel with a sore arm the following season.

The 1965 season saw the Red Sox lose 100 games, finish ninth, and suffer an attendance drop to 652,201, their lowest since wartime 1945. For Tom Yawkey, it was the longest and dreariest summer he had endured as club owner. The team led the league with 165 home runs, including 32 by Conigliaro, who at the age of twenty became the youngest home-run leader in league history. But the club, under Billy Herman, did not play well, making the second most errors (162), while the pitchers logged the highest ERA (4.24) and allowed the most

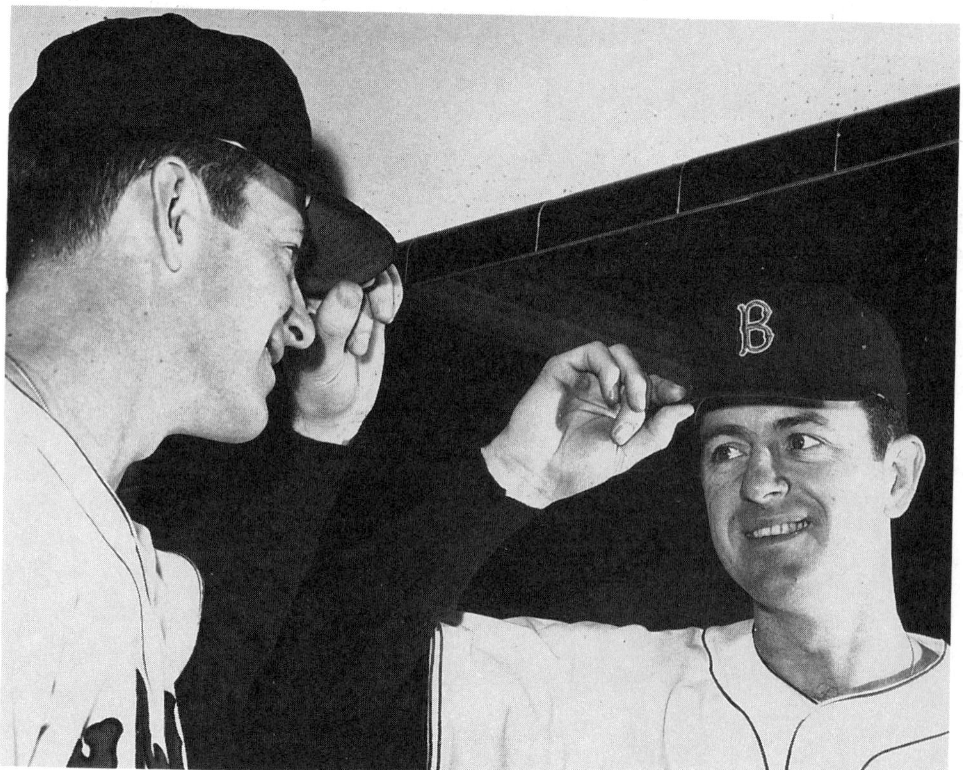

The colorful, power-hitting Dick Stuart checking himself out. He played for the Sox in 1963 and 1964, with two-year totals of 75 home runs and 232 RBIs, but they weren't enough to offset his fielding deficiencies, and he was soon traded.

Boston's 1963 infield. *Left to right:* Frank Malzone, Eddie Bressoud, Chuck Schilling, and Dick Stuart.

runs (791). Still, there were a few positive signs, most notably from young shortstop Rico Petrocelli and right-hander Jim Lonborg, who impressed a lot of people despite a 9–17 record.

The club started out the 1966 season showing little improvement, going 27–47 over its first seventy-four games. But then, Herman said, "Things began to change. We started putting it together. It was too late for any kind of pennant race, but over the second half we played pretty decent ball." From July on, the Sox were 45–43, but despite this they finished ninth again.

The club had shown a definite spark in the second half of the 1966 season, but after two ninth-place finishes in a row, not even the most optimistic Fenway diehard could have anticipated what was going to happen in 1967—the year of the Impossible Dream.

The Red Sox had a new manager in 1967. Dick Williams was a thirty-eight-year-old former ballplayer who had made the big-league tour with Brooklyn, Baltimore, Cleveland, Kansas City, and finally Boston, with whom he ended his playing days in 1964. A .260 lifetime hitter for his thirteen big-league seasons, Williams had always been a sharp observer of the game, one who had been grooming himself for a managerial career ever since his playing days had begun to wane.

To Dick Williams, winning baseball was more than base hits and runs batted in; baseball was a game of component parts, and each had to be executed efficiently: run-downs, relays, cut-offs, hitting behind the runner, bunting. To Williams, one rusty or ill-working cog could impair the entire machine. He was relentless in his insistence that the game be played his way; he could be caustic in expressing himself, to umpires and opponents as well as his own players.

Dick Radatz (1962–66).

"Mental mistakes I can't tolerate," he said. "A man has to know what he's got to do on the field at all times, and it's got to be automatic. Missing a cut-off man looks like a physical action; to me it's a mental mistake. It shouldn't happen. I can't tolerate a guy missing a sign. I won't tolerate it."

He began drilling his men in spring training, driving them hard, goading and haranguing them.

Felix Mantilla. The ex–National Leaguer played infield and outfield for Boston from 1963 to 1965. He hit 30 home runs in 1964. (*Courtesy NBL*)

"The players probably thought I was crazy as a loon," he said. "But, hell, I had a one-year contract. So if I was crazy, I was going to be crazy all year and give it the best I had. Frankly, I didn't make too many friends among the players that year. . . . I don't care if they like me or not. I am concerned, though, about them respecting my knowledge of the game. If they do, they'll play for me, and they'll play at the top of their ability."

They played for Williams in 1967, surprising the rest of the league, their fans, and probably themselves. It was a ten-team league then, and four of those teams scrambled through one of the most engrossing pennant races of all time: the Detroit Tigers, Minnesota Twins, Chicago White Sox, and the Red Sox, who in spring training were listed as 100–1 shots.

(OPPOSITE PAGE) Tony Conigliaro (*left*) (1964–67, 1969–70, 1975) and Tony Horton (1964–67). A first baseman, Horton was traded in 1967 to Cleveland, where he had some good years.

It was the year that Carl Yastrzemski won the Triple Crown with 44 home runs (tying Harmon Killebrew), 121 RBIs, and a .326 batting average. Yastrzemski's hitting was extraordinary at

(Top left)
Dave Morehead (1963–68) after pitching his no-hitter against Cleveland at Fenway on September 15, 1965.

(Top right)
Carl Yastrzemski.

(Bottom left)
Billy Herman, who managed the Red Sox in 1965–66.

(Bottom right)
Infielder Dalton Jones (1964–69). He hit .289 in his best year—1967, the year of the Impossible Dream.
(Courtesy NBL)

a time when pitching dominated—Boston's .255 team average was high in a league that averaged just .236 overall. At bat and in the field, Yaz performed all year long with white-hot intensity, putting together a legendary season, one in which Dick Williams described him as "the greatest ballplayer I ever saw."

Dick Williams, Red Sox manager from 1967 to 1969.

Outside of Yastrzemski and Jim Lonborg, who was 22–9, this pennant-winning Red Sox club was not very prepossessing. First baseman George Scott turned in a good year with 19 home runs and a .303 average, while second baseman Mike Andrews, shortstop Rico Petrocelli, and third baseman Joe Foy hit moderately well. The talented rookie outfielder Reggie Smith batted .246, and the catching was handled by weak-hitting Mike Ryan and Russ Gibson, with late-season help from the veteran Elston Howard, acquired from the Yankees.

Another packed house at Fenway.

First baseman George Scott (1966–71, 1977–79). He hit 33 home runs in 1977.

The Red Sox victory in 1967 was all the more remarkable when one considers the loss of Tony Conigliaro. On August 18, Tony C was injured, almost fatally, when a high inside pitch from California's Jack Hamilton carried up and struck him on the left side of the face. The impact fractured his cheekbone, dislocated his jaw, and damaged the retina of his left eye. Under this shattering pain, his mind swooning with shock and fear, Conigliaro thought he was going to die. He didn't die, but his baseball career lay in ruins. He missed the rest of the season and all of 1968 because of vision problems. He came back in 1969 and for two years played well, hitting 36 homers in 1970, but problems with his vision recurred and he was forced to retire.

Behind Lonborg and his 22 wins were right-handers Gary Bell and Jose Santiago, with 12 each, and relief ace John Wyatt, with 10 (and 20 saves). Some people said it was as unimpressive a staff as ever won a pennant, but, it might be pointed out, in 1951, 1952, and 1956 the Indians had three twenty-game winners on the staff each year and finished second each time.

When he took over the team, Williams had said only, "We'll

Jim Lonborg (1965–71). Boston's first Cy Young Award winner.

Right-hander Gary Bell (1967–68), who contributed a 12–8 record to the 1967 pennant.

win more games than we'll lose." Through the end of June he was right, but just barely, the team mounting a 37–34 record. But then, with Yastrzemski playing with splendid fury and Lonborg becoming a true ace, the Red Sox kept improving: In July they were 19–10; in August, 20–15; and then coming down the hot coals of the pennant stretch, 15–11.

With just a handful of games remaining, four teams were still in contention. The White Sox, with the league's best pitching offset by a .225 club batting average, were the first to be eliminated. In the final two games of the season, the Red Sox eliminated the Twins at Fenway, then hurried to the clubhouse to listen to radio accounts of the Tigers losing to the Angels, which prevented a Boston-Detroit deadlock and gave the Red Sox their first pennant in twenty-one years.

The final game, in which Boston beat Minnesota 5–3, was a microcosm of the Fenway season—Lonborg pitching the crucial victory and Yastrzemski ripping clutch hits, driving home vital runs, and chilling a Minnesota rally with a great throw from left field. Getting better and better as the late-September pressure mounted, Yastrzemski had 23 hits in his last 44 at-bats, 10 for his last 13, 7 for his last 8, and 4 for 4 on the final day. In other words, as things got tougher, he got better.

The 1967 World Series was in many ways a replay of the outstanding 1946 pageant: The Sox played the Cardinals, the Cards won in seven, and a star Cardinal pitcher rang up three wins.

Despite being emotionally drained from the intensity of their storybook finish, the Red Sox found the resources to extend the Cardinals to the distance before finally bowing out. Boston's primary problem in the Series was named Bob Gibson, not only one of the great pitchers of his or any other age, but in World Series competition simply overpowering. The Red Sox also ran into a blazing-hot Lou Brock and another hot hitter with a familiar face, ex-Yankee Roger Maris (who in 1961 had hit his historic sixty-first home run off Red Sox right-hander Tracy Stallard). Brock rapped twelve hits in the seven

A familiar tableau in 1967: Yastrzemski is being greeted after hitting one of his 44 home runs. That's Reggie Smith on the left and Mike Andrews on the right.

games, batted .414, and stole a record seven bases, while Maris had ten hits, batted .385, and drove in seven runs.

Because he had worked the final game of the season, Lonborg was not ready to open the Series for Boston; Jose Santiago did and pitched well, but Gibson was better, winning 2–1 at Fenway. Lonborg was ready for Game 2 and was scintillating, firing a one-hitter, as Boston won, 5–0, with Yastrzemski (who had ten hits and a .400 average for the Series) clubbing two home runs.

(Opposite page) Carl Yastrzemski, Triple Crown winner in 1967.

St. Louis took Game 3, 5–2, and Game 4, 6–0, with Gibson throwing the shutout. Down three games to one, the Red Sox fought back. Lonborg pitched a 3–1 three-hitter in Game 5, and Boston then evened the Series in Game 6, 8–4, boosted by a brace of Petrocelli homers. Game 7, however, was all St. Louis and Gibson. The hard-throwing Cardinal right-hander delivered his third complete-game victory of the Series, defeating a tired Lonborg (working on two days' rest) by a 7–2 score.

For Red Sox fans, the World Series defeat did not carry as much sting as these disappointments usually do.

"That pennant was so unexpected and so exhilarating," one Boston fan said, "that we were still celebrating it after the Series was over. Sure, the Series loss made us sick, but it was the kind of sickness you feel when you've had an overly rich dessert after a hearty meal."

John Wyatt (1966–68), Boston's bullpen strongman in 1967. He won 10 games and saved 20.

Ken Harrelson scoring in a cloud of dust as Athletics catcher Dave Duncan reaches for the high throw. No. 7 is Reggie Smith. The umpire is Lou DiMuro. Harrelson (1967–69) led the league in RBIs in 1968.

Mike Andrews (1966–70), second baseman on the 1967 pennant winners. His best year was 1969, when he batted .293.

It's the final game of the 1967 season—a "must" win for Boston—and Yastrzemski has just drilled a clutch two-run single up the middle in the last of the sixth inning. A jacketed Jim Lonborg is about to head down the line at third.

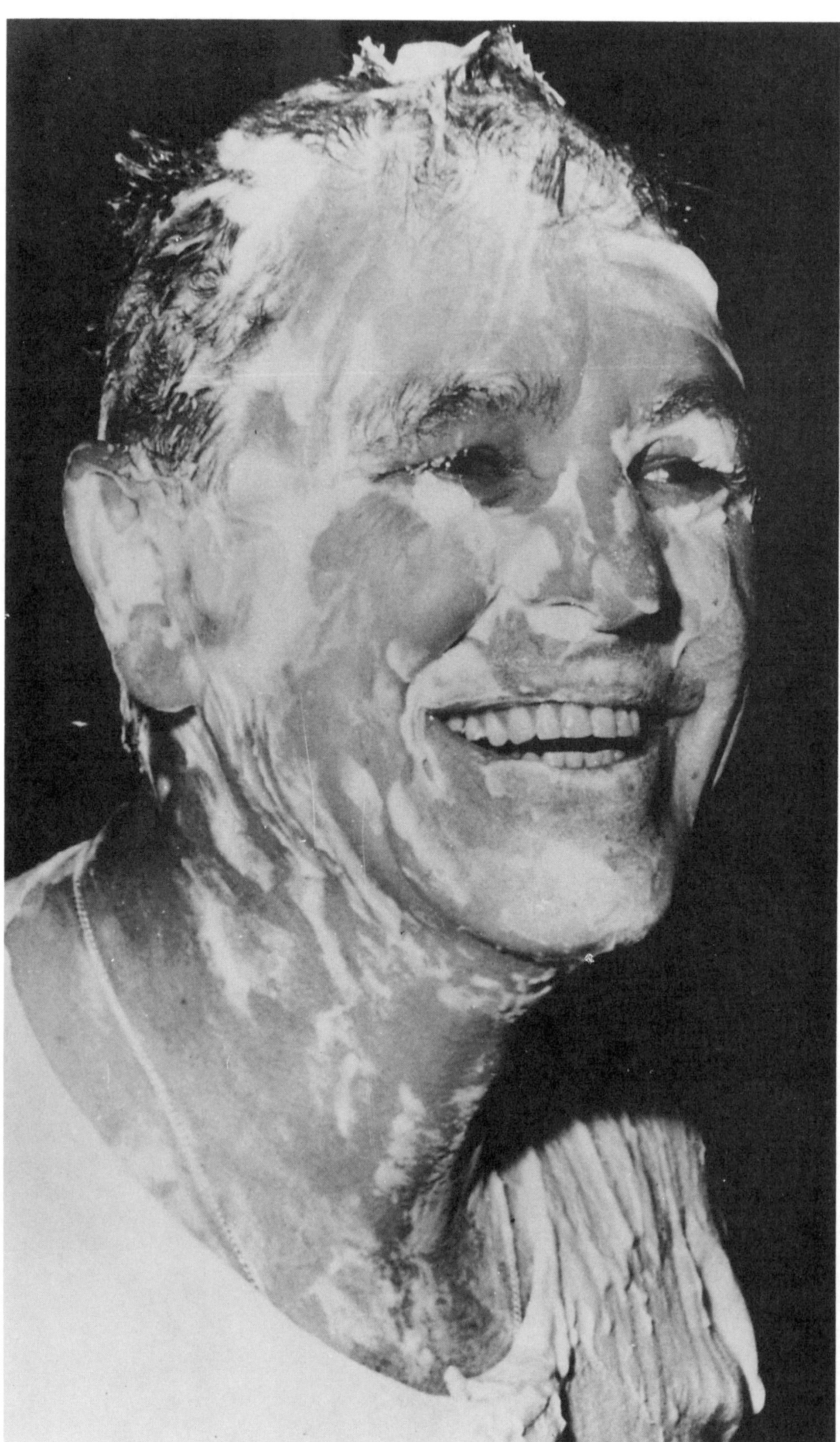

Dick Williams wearing "victory makeup"—a face covered with shaving cream smeared on by his players after the Red Sox had clinched the 1967 pennant.

The starting pitchers for the opening game of the 1967 World Series: the Cardinals' Bob Gibson (*left*) and Boston's Jose Santiago. Santiago (1966–70) contributed a 12–4 record in 1967.

Series star Lou Brock loses his cap as he sets out to steal third in the fifth inning of the seventh game of the 1967 Series. Jim Lonborg has just delivered the pitch.

There were some postseason badges to be awarded. Yastrzemski brought the club its fifth MVP Award and Lonborg became the first Red Sox pitcher to win a Cy Young plaque.

Jim Lonborg. *(Courtesy NBL)*

The long, sweet night of the Impossible Dream ended abruptly on December 23, on snowy mountain slopes near Nevada's Lake Tahoe, when Lonborg tore ligaments in his left knee in a skiing accident. The twenty-five-year-old right-hander was never the same pitcher again. He was 6–10 in 1968, 7–11 in 1969, and in 1970–71 won just fourteen games, after which he was traded to Milwaukee. He had some decent years pitching for Milwaukee, and later the Philadelphia Phillies, but was never again the overpowering pitcher he had been in 1967.

Right-hander Ray Culp (1968–73), who was 16–6 in 1968 and 17–8 the next year.

The Sox finished fourth in 1968. This was the "Year of the Pitcher," when the American League batted an all-time low .230. There was just one .300 hitter in the league, Carl Yastrzemski, whose .301 remains the lowest average ever for a batting champion. It was Yaz's third title. Boston also had the RBI leader in Ken Harrelson (109), who had been picked up as a free agent the previous August after being let go by the Athletics in a dispute with owner Charles Finley. The pennant afterglow remained an aura over Fenway all summer, however, as the club set a new attendance record of 1,940,788.

Three consecutive third-place finishes followed in 1969, 1970, and 1971, the Sox never getting closer than eighteen games to Earl Weaver's Baltimore Orioles, who ran off with three easy pennants. A highlight for Red Sox fans came in 1969, when Rico Petrocelli's 40 home runs set a new record for American League shortstops (Yastrzemski also hit 40 that year), breaking by one the record Vern Stephens had set with Boston in 1949.

Dick Williams was let go at the end of the 1969 season, replaced by Eddie Kasko, who ran the team for four years. In 1970, Yastrzemski missed a fourth batting title by the width of a gnat's eyelash, finishing at .3286 to .3289 for the winner,

Former Yankee catcher Elston Howard joined the Sox late in 1967 and was with them through the 1968 season. Here he has just gloved the peg home and is about to lay it on Chicago's Luis Aparicio.

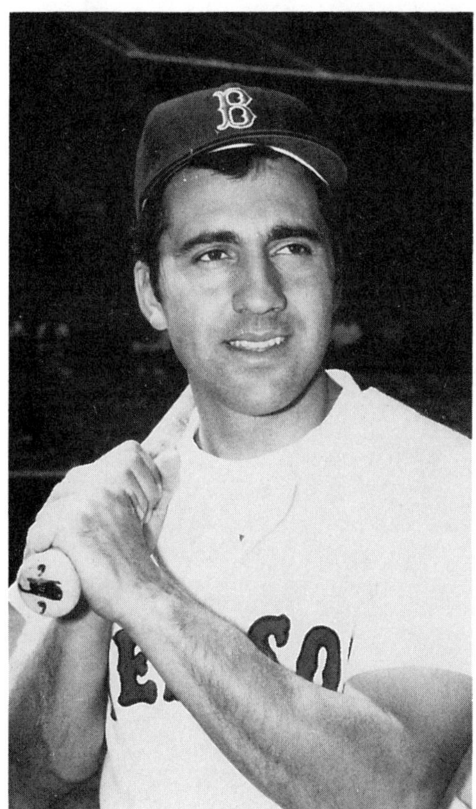

(LEFT)
Rico Petrocelli (1963, 1965–76). His 40 home runs in 1969 are the record for an American League shortstop.

(RIGHT)
The talented Reggie Smith (1966–73). The switch-hitting outfielder led the league in doubles in 1968 and 1971, when he also hit 30 home runs. He hit .300 three times for Boston.

(TOP LEFT)
Sonny Siebert (1969–73). The big right-hander was 15–8 in 1970, 16–10 a year later.

(TOP RIGHT)
Eddie Kasko, Red Sox manager from 1970 to 1973.

(BOTTOM LEFT)
Luis Aparicio (1971–73). One of the greatest defensive shortstops of all time, Luis is shown here firing to first base to complete a double play on Detroit's Dick McAuliffe. The sliding baserunner is Ed Brinkman.

(BOTTOM RIGHT)
Gary Peters (1970–72). The longtime White Sox ace lefty finished up with Boston. He was 16–11 in 1970.

California's Alex Johnson. Ironically, it was the highest average of Yaz's twenty-three-year career.

The 1972 season began for Boston with an unfortunate trade, was followed by a brief strike by major-league players, and ended for the Red Sox with one of the game's outstanding baserunners falling down and perhaps costing the club a division title.

Second baseman Doug Griffin (1971–77). He was never the same after a severe beaning by Nolan Ryan.

With George Scott having been traded to Milwaukee as part of a nine-player deal (Lonborg also went, with Boston getting pitcher Marty Pattin and outfielder Tommy Harper, among others), the Sox needed a first baseman. The man they wanted was the Yankees' Danny Cater. The man they traded for him was left-hander Sparky Lyle, who in five years had established himself as one of the league's better bullpen artists. And, as in the days of yore, Boston got skinned in a Yankee deal—Cater doing very little for Boston and Lyle going on to help the Yankees win three pennants.

Bob Montgomery (1970–79). An excellent backup catcher, Montgomery later became part of Boston's TV announcing crew. *(Courtesy NBL)*

The players' strike chopped some games from the schedule at the beginning of the year, games that were never made up. Boston missed seven games, and Detroit, the team they fought down to the end, missed six.

Going into Detroit for their final three games of the season, the Sox were a half-game ahead of the Tigers. In the opener, the Tigers held a 1–0 lead in the top of the third when Harper and Luis Aparicio led off with singles. (Aparicio had been acquired in December 1970 from the White Sox. He had led the league in stolen bases nine straight times.) Yastrzemski then drove one over the center fielder's head. Harper scored and Aparicio should have, but the usually nimble-footed veteran stumbled and fell while rounding third, got up but only to stumble again and fall. By this time Yastrzemski had arrived at the bag, With two men on third, Yaz was tagged out. Reggie Smith then fanned and the rally was snuffed.

The aborted rally proved to be Boston's best shot at Tiger lefty Mickey Lolich, who took advantage of the escape and went on to beat the Sox, 4–1. Detroit won again the next day,

(Left)
Sparky Lyle (1967–71). He followed the old trail to New York.

(Right)
Danny Cater (1972–74). Danny batted .313 as a part-timer in 1973, but quickly faded out.

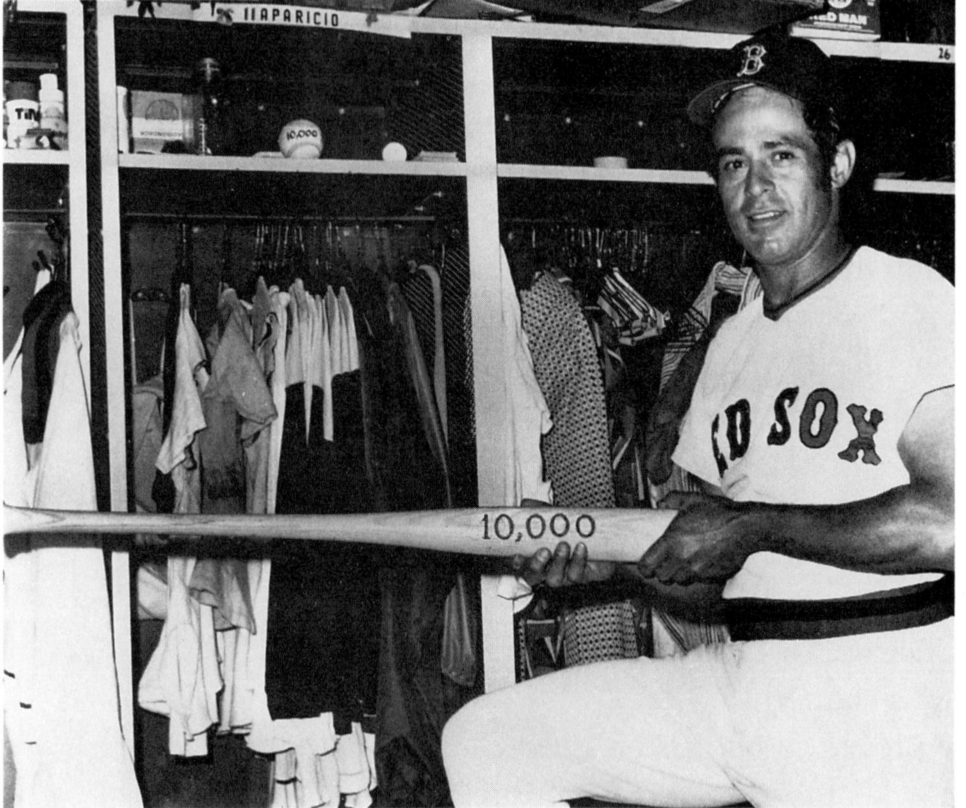

Luis Aparacio celebrating his 10,000th big-league at-bat. He is one of only fourteen big leaguers to have that many official at-bats.

3–1, and clinched the division. Boston's victory on the final day only meant that they had lost by a half-game margin, Detroit having played one more game and won it, this irregularity caused by the strike.

Though Marty Pattin led the staff with 17 wins, the most striking pitching done in Boston that year was by right-hander Luis Tiant, a reclamation project. After some outstanding seasons with Cleveland, arm miseries had sent Tiant to the minors, from where Boston snatched him in 1971. Despite a 1–7 record that year, the Sox stayed with him. He was 15–6 in 1972, with a league-leading 1.91 ERA (including, at one point, 42⅓ consecutive scoreless innings), the first Red Sox pitcher since Carl Mays in 1917 to record an ERA under 2.00.

Another individual success story was a twenty-three-year-old rookie catcher named Carlton Fisk. Big, strong, ruggedly good-looking, Fisk never displayed any freshman diffidence but was immediately in charge behind the plate. Any pitcher, veteran or not, who was not bearing down to the young catcher's satisfaction was apt to receive a visit to the mound and then a stern lecture, or, if not that, then a return throw that was like a line drive. In his first full season, Fisk batted .293, hit 22

(LEFT)
Marty Pattin (1972–73). They called this tough right-hander "the Bulldog." He was 17–13 in 1972. Boston traded him to Kansas City for Dick Drago.

(RIGHT)
Left-hander John Curtis (1970–73). He was 11–8 in 1972.

The speedy Juan Beniquez (1971–72, 1974–75) is beating the play at home. Juan came up as a shortstop but later switched to the outfield.

Outfielder Ben Oglivie (1971–73) came up with the Red Sox but became a league-leading home-run hitter with Milwaukee.

Luis Aparicio has just risen to his feet after stumbling at third base in Boston's crucial late-season game with Detroit—only to find Carl Yastrzemski arriving there. Yaz was ruled out. The umpire is Lou DiMuro.

Carlton Fisk (1969, 1971–80).

home runs, and tied for the league lead with nine triples, making him the only American League catcher ever to lead in three-baggers. For his work, he was voted Rookie of the Year, the third Red Sox player to earn the distinction.

— 11 —

A Burst of Talent

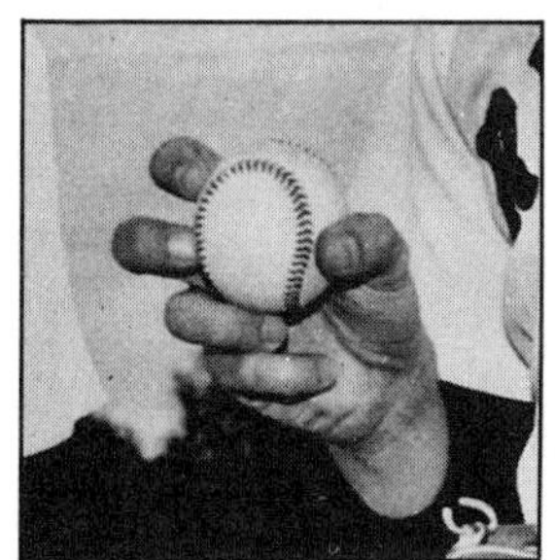

The Sox finished second again in 1973, eight games behind the Orioles. Tiant rang up a 20–13 record, and Harper set a new club record with 54 stolen bases. Orlando Cepeda, the only full-time designated hitter the club has ever had, hit 20 homers and batted .289. (The former National League star played just that one year for Boston.) Platooning in the outfield was twenty-one-year-old Dwight Evans, who batted just .223 but displayed some power with 10 home runs, as well as superb defensive abilities and a cannonlike throwing arm. It was the beginning of one of the great careers in Red Sox history.

Despite finishing third twice and second twice, Kasko was gone after the 1973 season and was replaced by Darrell Johnson, a poker-faced former backup catcher with seven big-league clubs.

The Red Sox finished third in the East in 1974, but now the club was beginning to glow with young talent. Along with Evans and Fisk, there were first baseman–designated hitter Cecil Cooper, shortstop Rick Burleson (good enough to move Petrocelli to third), and, brought up at the end of the year, a pair of young outfielders named Fred Lynn and Jim Rice. Tiant was 22–13, the first Red Sox pitcher since Ferriss in 1945–46 to have back-to-back twenty-game seasons, and the free-spirited but talented left-hander Bill Lee was 17–15. Right-hander Rick Wise (acquired from the Cardinals along with outfielder Bernie Carbo and right-hander Reggie Cleveland in a ten-player swap that saw the departure of Reggie Smith) was held by a sore arm to a 3–4 season but was going to do better. The Boston farm system had produced a remarkable number of stars and budding stars who were going to give the city its first pennant in eight years.

Darrell Johnson's 1975 club took the East Division title by four and a half games over the Orioles. The Sox moved into first place in early June and never relinquished it, thanks to one of their best-balanced teams ever.

(Opposite page) Rookie outfielder Dwight Evans in 1973. (*Courtesy NBL*)

(TOP LEFT)
Orlando Cepeda, Boston's DH in 1973, his only year with the team.

(TOP RIGHT)
Luis Tiant (1971–78), a twenty-game winner in 1973, 1974, and 1976.

(BOTTOM LEFT)
Outfielder Tommy Harper (1972–74) whose 54 stolen bases in 1973 remain the Boston club record.

(BOTTOM RIGHT)
Darrell Johnson, Red Sox manager from 1974 to 1976.

With Evans, Lynn, and Rice forming one of the great outfields in Red Sox history, Yastrzemski was moved to first base. Petrocelli was at third, the hard-as-nails Burleson at short, and, at second, a midseason acquisition from California, Denny Doyle. Fisk, missing half the season with injuries, was backed up by Bob Montgomery and Tim Blackwell, with Cooper filling in at DH and first base.

For a change, Boston pitching was deep in quality. Wise was 19–12; Tiant, 18–14; Lee, 17–9; lefty Roger Moret, 14–3; and Cleveland, 13–9. They were backed up by bullpen ace Dick Drago.

Lynn and Rice—the "Gold Dust Twins"—had memorable rookie seasons. Lynn batted .331, hit 21 homers and a league-high 47 doubles, drove in 105 runs, and led with a .566 slugging average. The twenty-three-year-old Californian with the smooth power swing and magic glove in center set a precedent by being voted both Rookie of the Year and Most Valuable Player. Rice, with the most ferocious right-handed power rip seen at Fenway since the days of Jimmie Foxx, hit 22 homers,

Moment of impact: Juan Beniquez has just made dubious contact, splitting his bat in two.

Carl Yastrzemski, who put in a lot of time at first base for the Red Sox, is taking a throw here in an attempt to pick off Cleveland's Duane Kuiper. Duane made it back safely. *(Photograph by Nancy Hogue)*

The "Gold Dust Twins" of 1975: Fred Lynn *(left)* and Jim Rice. *(Courtesy NBL)*

drove in 102 runs, and batted .309. Fisk batted .331; Cooper, .311; Doyle, .310. The team's .275 batting average was the league's best since 1956.

Lynn put on the year's single biggest one-man explosion in Detroit on the night of June 18, hitting three home runs, a triple, and a single, tying the league record for total bases in a game.

Denny Doyle (1975–77), second baseman on the 1975 pennant winners.

Boston tore through their first League Championship Series with minimum effort, sweeping three-time world champion Oakland in three straight. (The LCS was then a best-of-five affair.) With Rice sidelined by a September hand injury, Yastrzemski took over in left field and performed brilliantly. Scenting pennant blood once more, the thirty-six-year-old veteran evoked memories of his landmark 1967 season with a .455 average in the Oakland series and such dazzling glovework that an awed Reggie Jackson (then with Oakland) said later, "From now on I'm calling him Mister."

Shortstop Rick Burleson (1974–80).

The October 1975 confrontation between Boston and Cincinnati has been called by many people the most memorable World Series ever, with a riveting Game 6 packaging baseball theatrics of the highest caliber.

These were the Cincinnati Reds of the "Big Red Machine," a club studded with future Hall of Famers. The primary dynamos of the machine were third baseman Pete Rose, catcher Johnny Bench, second baseman Joe Morgan, first baseman Tony Perez, shortstop Dave Concepcion, and outfielders George Foster and Ken Griffey. Starting pitchers Don Gullett, Gary Nolan, and Jack Billingham were backed up by an unusually deep corps of relievers in Pedro Borbon, Clay Carroll, Will McEnaney, and Rawley Eastwick. All of this talent was shrewdly and prudently manipulated by Sparky Anderson.

Cincinnati had not won a World Series since 1940; Boston, not since 1918. As these two fine clubs lined up at Fenway for their Game 1 introductions, one sportswriter, gazing down at the remarkable array of talent, said, "It's a shame one of them is

Carlton Fisk.
(*Photograph by Ronald C. Modra*)

going to have to lose." By the time it was over, however, he was close to being wrong, for there was universal agreement that, while Cincinnati won, Boston did not lose.

Tiant put the Red Sox one up by shutting down the Reds, 6–0, in the opener, Boston scoring all of its runs in the last of the seventh. In Game 2, Bill Lee took a 2–1 lead into the top of the ninth, only to see the Reds score twice and get away with a 3–2 win, tying the Series.

Bernie Carbo trying to get around Detroit's John Wockenfuss and score, but the umpire looks ready to thumb him out. No. 14 is Jim Rice.

Luis Tiant, one of the most popular of all Red Sox players.

Reggie Cleveland (*left*) and Rick Wise, a pair of Boston's right-handed starters. Cleveland (1974–78) was 13–9 in 1975, while Wise (1974–77) was 19–12 in that pennant year.

Game 3, in Cincinnati, was another thriller; it also featured one of the most controversial plays in Series history. Trailing 5–1 after five innings, Boston fought back to tie it on a Dwight Evans home run in the top of the ninth. In the bottom of the tenth, Cesar Geronimo opened with a single. Anderson sent Ed Armbrister up to bunt. The ball was laid down in front of the plate. Fisk was out of the chute in a flash, so quickly that he got tangled up with Armbrister, who was slow getting out of the batter's box. Thus impeded, Fisk, who had a probable double play in front of him, fired the ball into center field, allowing Geronimo to go to third and Armbrister to second.

Dick Drago (1974–75, 1978–80), for several years Boston's top reliever.

It was clearly a case of interference, at least to everyone in the Red Sox dugout and to all of New England. Umpire Larry Barnett, however, ruled it a "collision" and not interference. Fisk and Darrell Johnson argued vehemently but futilely. The call stood. After an intentional walk and a strikeout, Morgan singled to center, giving the Reds a 6–5 victory.

Tiant brought the Sox even at two games apiece with an epic 5–4 victory in which the tough and wily Cuban threw 163 pitches. The Reds took Game 5 by a 6–2 score, and then the clubs headed back to Boston for "the greatest game ever played."

Hard-throwing left-hander Roger Moret (1970–1975) didn't pitch a lot for Boston, but when he did he was almost unbeatable. His record with the Sox was 41–18.

Game 6 of the 1975 World Series remains the game that future World Series thrillers will have to be measured against. It was Tiant against Nolan (the travel date plus three days of rain enabled Johnson to bring back his ace), but by the time it was over, four hours later, Anderson had used eight pitchers and Johnson four, new standards of tension and excitement had been reached, and New England was drenched in emotion.

Fred Lynn put the Sox up, 3–0, with a three-run rocket in the last of the first. But by the bottom of the eighth inning some steady Cincinnati sharpshooting had riddled Boston, and the Reds had a 6–3 lead. The Red Sox had two men on base when Johnson sent Bernie Carbo up to pinch-hit. Carbo, who had come up through the Cincinnati farm system, had pinch-hit a

Action in Game 3 of the 1975 League Championship Series between Boston and Oakland, at Oakland. Fred Lynn is sliding safely into second as second baseman Phil Garner reaches for the throw. Lynn had lined to left fielder Claudell Washington, who dropped the ball. The umpire is Jim Evans. Boston's 5–3 victory in this game gave them the pennant.

(Opposite page)
Jim Rice, Boston's greatest right-handed hitter since Foxx.

home run earlier in the Series, and Red Sox fans were asking him to do it again. It was asking a lot, but this was not the real world—it was the universe of baseball, and Bernie lit it up by crashing a game-tying three-run homer into the center-field bleachers. It was now six all.

In the bottom of the ninth, the Sox loaded the bases with none out, only to allow the Reds to shake free when George Foster took Lynn's fly ball along the left-field line and threw Doyle out at the plate. Boston did not score. Often, when a team does not score after having its opponent so decisively impaled, it is a bad omen. But this was a night when miracles crackled like thunderbolts through the New England skies.

In the top of the eleventh, one of the thunderbolts struck right field. With one out and Griffey on first, Morgan ripped one toward the right-field seats that was seemingly ticketed for glory. But the glory lay in Dwight Evans's glove. The right fielder ran back and made a spectacular on-the-run leaping grab

Bill Lee delivering the first pitch of Game 2 of the 1975 World Series. The batter is Cincinnati's Pete Rose.

Cincinnati's George Foster is stealing second in Game 3 of the 1975 Series. The ball skipped past Denny Doyle and Foster went on to third.

The Boston Red Sox ballet troupe performing during the fourth game of the 1975 World Series. Trying in vain to catch Dave Concepcion's bloop double in the fourth inning are (*left to right*) left fielder Juan Beniquez, shortstop Rick Burleson, and center fielder Fred Lynn.

of the ball just before it would have become a home run. Evans then compounded the felony by firing into the infield and doubling up Griffey, who never thought the catch could be made.

The game rolled on to the bottom of the twelfth inning, locked in a 6–6 tie. Playing extra innings in Fenway is like skating on ever-thinning ice.

Fisk was the first man up for Boston in the bottom of the twelfth. He wasted no time, lofting the first pitch from right-hander Pat Darcy high along the left-field line. There was no question about distance, only whether it was fair or foul. Fisk stood at home plate pushing his arms through the air toward fair territory, trying to guide the ball. Then he began bouncing up and down along the first-base line, still trying to wigwag the ball fair. With the undoubted help of his waving, the ball struck the foul pole, and, like a man given an electric shock, Fisk leaped into the air, and all of Fenway with him. The Series was now knotted at three games apiece.

Fisk–Ed Armbrister collision in the bottom of the tenth inning of Game 3 of the 1975 Series. Plate umpire Larry Barnett said it was not interference. New England disagreed.

Carlton Fisk confiding to Larry Barnett what really happened.

Bernie Carbo launching the missile that electrified New England in the bottom of the eighth inning of Game 6.

Game 7 couldn't compete with its immediate predecessor, despite the weight of finality it carried. It was a good game, a one-run nail-biter that wasn't decided until the top of the ninth. It was as if destiny could not make up its mind which of these two finely balanced ball clubs should be crowned champion and waited until the last possible moment before filing a decision.

It was left-handers Lee and Gullett on the mound to start. Boston took a three-run lead in the bottom of the third, but never scored again. Cincinnati got two in the sixth, tied it in the seventh, and scored 1975's ultimate run in the top of the ninth on a bloop single by Morgan.

It was the third straight seven-game Series for Boston, and again they had fallen short. For New England, however, the glory of Game 6 was a hearth at which to warm itself throughout the winter.

Bernie Carbo (1974–78). (*Courtesy NBL*)

Another highlight of the memorable Game 6 of the 1975 Series: Dwight Evans about to leave his feet and snare Joe Morgan's bid for a home run in the top of the eleventh inning. Evans then turned it into a double play by firing in and nailing Ken Griffey, who had gone almost to third base.

(OPPOSITE PAGE) Carlton Fisk trying to communicate with the ball he has just lofted toward the Wall in the bottom of the twelfth inning of Game 6. He got through.

27
27

The 1976 season was for Boston fans one of peculiarities and of sadness. After getting off to a slow start, the Red Sox on June 15 made the largest cash transaction in baseball history by buying relief ace Rollie Fingers and outfielder Joe Rudi from Oakland for $2 million. At the same time, George Steinbrenner gave Oakland a reported $1.5 million for left-hander Vida Blue. (Unwilling to pay the salaries they would be demanding and fearful of losing his stars to free agency with no return, Oakland owner Charles Finley had decided to cash in his bluest chips.)

But Fingers and Rudi never played a game for Boston, nor did Blue for New York. Commissioner Bowie Kuhn voided the transactions, citing the "best interests of baseball." (An irate Finley later challenged Kuhn's ruling in court, but lost.)

The attempted purchase of Fingers and Rudi was Tom Yawkey's farewell gesture on behalf of his ball club. On July 9, 1976, the seventy-three-year-old Yawkey died of leukemia. During his forty-four-year ownership, Yawkey had built his beloved team from chronic losers to one of baseball's most glamorous franchises. Always a fan first and owner second, he was one of the last of a vanishing breed, a man who cared about his players—both during their careers and after. It was said that he was too sentimental about his players and that he pampered and overpaid them (of no other owner in the history of baseball has this ever been said). The man whose fortune was counted in the hundreds of millions was remembered by those who knew him as quiet and modest—"a regular guy," said a longtime Fenway employee. Times changed, but Tom Yawkey never did.

With the club riding a 41–45 record after eighty-six games, Darrell Johnson learned just how tenuous the job of big-league manager could be. Less than a year after winning a pennant and missing a world championship by the slimmest of margins, Johnson was let out, replaced by third-base coach Don Zimmer. Zimmer was a feisty former infielder and previously manager at San Diego. The little round man would have fine winning records in Boston—97–64, 99–64, 91–69—but never took home the big cigar.

Boston finished third in 1976, and after the season made what would turn out to be a poor trade. Opting for right-handed power, they dealt Cecil Cooper to Milwaukee for their former first baseman George Scott. Scott had one good year, in 1977, and then faded out, while Cooper went on to stardom with the Brewers, batting over .300 for seven straight years.

The era of free agency and instant millionaires was now upon baseball, and Boston entered the market in November 1976 by signing right-handed reliever Bill Campbell (who was leaving Minnesota) to a five-year contract. The economic transition in baseball was this abrupt: In 1976, the Twins had paid Campbell $22,000; the Red Sox' contract called for more than $1 million (and it wasn't long before this pay scale was to look paltry).

The Sox won 97 games in 1977, tying Baltimore for second place in the East, two and a half games behind the Yankees. It was the best victory total by a Red Sox team since the 104 taken by the 1946 pennant winners.

Cecil Cooper (1971–76) (*left*) getting some insights from coach Johnny Pesky.

Dwight Evans examining the helmet he was wearing when he was hit in the head and knocked unconscious by a pitch thrown by Seattle pitcher Mike Parrott in late August 1978. The split helmet indicates the force of the ball's impact.

The club was reminiscent of some former Red Sox teams—long on power but short on pitching. They clouted an all-time club-record 213 home runs, fourth highest total in American League history. Jim Rice hit 39, tops in the league, followed by Scott's 33, 30 by young third baseman Butch Hobson, 28 by Yastrzemski, and 26 by Fisk. Hobson, Fisk, Rice, and Yastrzemski each drove in more than 100 runs. The staff's top winner, however, was Campbell, with 13, all of them earned in relief. Campbell also led the league with 31 saves; it was, however, the only truly productive year he gave Boston, as arm miseries plagued him during his four remaining seasons with the club.

Butch Hobson (1975–80). In 1977, Butch hit 30 home runs and drove in 112 runs.

In 1978, Zimmer got the team off to an awesome start. They were 23–7 in May and 18–7 in June and by July 19 had a 62–29 record, a .681 winning percentage that saw them ten games ahead of second-place Milwaukee and fourteen in front of the fourth-place Yankees. The New Yorkers were riddled with injuries and smoldering with dissension. In late July, the Yankees changed managers, Billy Martin leaving (it was the first of his five managerial departures from the Yankees) and Bob Lemon taking over. For the Yankees, it was a crucial change, for Lemon soothed the troubled waters, got his injured players back, and set the club on a .700 course (48–20) for the rest of the season, making an irresistible advance that gradually eroded the Red Sox' lead.

Boston had put together one of the strongest teams in its history. Rice, Lynn, and Evans remained a potent outfield; Scott and Yastrzemski shared first base, Burleson was at short, Hobson at third, and at second was Jerry Remy, acquired from California. Fisk was guiding a staff that included two new

Butch Hobson sliding safely into home. The catcher is Milwaukee's Charley Moore. *(Photograph by Ronald C. Modra)*

starters in Dennis Eckersley, who had come from Cleveland in a trade, and Mike Torrez, who had left the Yankees to come to Boston as a free agent. In addition to these two right-handers there was Tiant, Lee, and reliever Bob Stanley, who was in his second season.

Bill Campbell (1977–81). *(Photograph by Nancy Hogue)*

The Sox were thriving under new ownership. In May, a group headed by Tom Yawkey's widow, Jean, Buddy LeRoux, and Haywood Sullivan had acquired the team for approximately $15 million. Mrs. Yawkey was installed as club president; LeRoux (who later sold out to his partners), formerly the team's trainer, was in charge of the business and administration portfolios; and Sullivan was responsible for player personnel. Sullivan's was a unique success story. In 1952, he had been signed by Boston for a large bonus. A catcher, he got into just sixty games for Boston over four years, then was traded to Kansas City, for whom he played until 1963. After closing out his playing career, he joined the Boston front office as vice-president in charge of player personnel, from there gradually rising to co-owner.

Bill Lee (1969–78). Lee was a 17-game winner in 1973, 1974, and 1975.

In July, the Red Sox stumbled to 13–15, while the Yankees under Lemon began their drive. Behind starters Ron Guidry, Ed Figueroa, and Catfish Hunter and relievers Goose Gossage and Sparky Lyle, New York won fifty-two of its last seventy-three, putting on one of the most sustained drives in baseball history. For Boston, the critical slide came between August 30 and September 16, when they lost fourteen of seventeen, including what has become known as the "Second Boston Massacre." The Yankees came to town, trailing by four, for a four-game series. The Red Sox proved much too hospitable to the visitors, losing by scores of 15–3, 13–2, 7–0, and 7–4.

(Opposite page)
Fred Lynn (1974–80). A superstar with Boston, Lynn was never the same lethal hitter after leaving Fenway.

After they fell out of first place by as many as three and a half games, Zimmer rallied his struggling troops for a stirring stretch run, winning eleven of the last thirteen, including the final seven in a row. When the final leaf of the schedule was

B
RED S

OSTON

turned, the Red Sox and the Yankees had identical (and impressive) 99–63 records, necessitating a one-game playoff for the division title.

(Opposite page)
Jim Rice: a left fielder in the tradition of Williams and Yastrzemski.
(Photograph by Ronald C. Modra)

By its very nature, it was going to be a historic game. And as the teams took the field at Fenway on the bright autumn afternoon of October 2, there was a sense that it was also going to be an unforgettable one; two superb units of players meeting for what was the most momentous game between their teams since the decisive final encounter that closed out the 1949 season.

◇ ◇ ◇

The Yankees started Guidry, who would end this season with a 25–3 record, while the Red Sox gave the ball to Torrez. Big Mike, putting his heart into every pitch, held the Yankees to just two hits over the first six innings, while his teammates

Dwight Evans is coming home in this July 1978 game against the Indians. The catcher is Gary Alexander.
(Photograph by Nancy Hogue)

were reaching Guidry for two runs, one of them on a Yastrzemski home run that barely wrapped itself around the right-field foul pole.

It remained 2–0, Boston, until the top of the seventh. Singles by Chris Chambliss and Roy White put the tying runs on with two out, with Bucky Dent coming up. Dent was a .240 hitter with just four home runs all season. He was by far the softest touch in the Yankee lineup, hardly the man you'd expect to spoil your afternoon, much less your entire summer.

Torrez delivered, and Dent hoisted a soft, high fly ball out toward left field. Torrez later said he thought it was "a routine fly ball ending the inning." And it was a routine fly ball—in any other park. But this was Fenway, where a neighborly left-field barrier inhales routine fly balls. Yastrzemski looked as though he might have a play on it. But he didn't. The ball had just enough pulse in it to putter through the air and drop into the screen for a three-run homer.

For historically minded Red Sox fans, the blow was reminiscent of another three-run hit by a light-hitting Yankee infielder that chilled the dreams of Boston fans—Jerry Coleman's bases-clearing double in the eighth inning of that 1949 season-closer. Like Dent's, Coleman's blow barely made a noise coming off the bat, but it sounded like a bass drum when it landed.

The Yankees scored another run in that inning, and another in the top of the eighth on a Reggie Jackson home run.

The Red Sox fought back. They pushed the score up to 5–4 and had the tying run at third with two out in the last of the ninth and Yastrzemski at bat. By now, the Yankees had Gossage on the mound, firing fastballs through the sound barrier. Yaz popped one of these bullets up in the air, and when it came down it was in the glove of third baseman Graig Nettles, and the season—for Boston—was over.

Ninety-nine victories—more than forty-five previous American League pennant winners had won—and the Red Sox finished second.

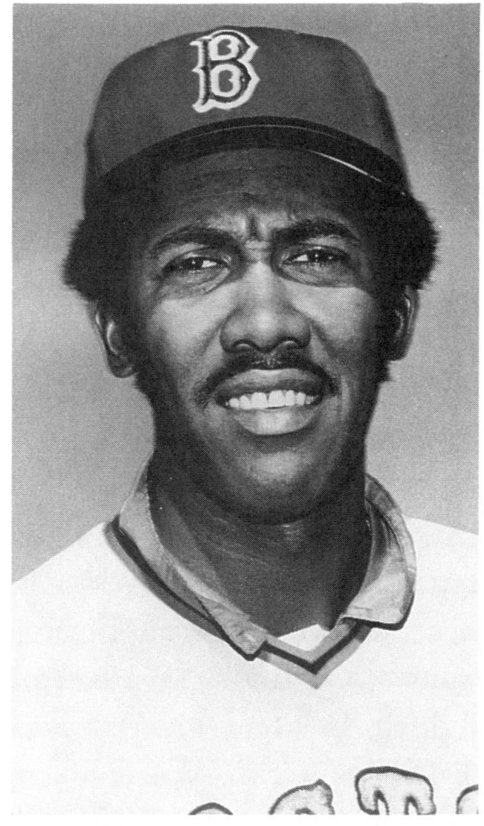

(TOP LEFT)
Dennis Eckersley pouring on the coal. Eckersley (1978–84) was 20–8 in 1978.
(Photograph by Nancy Hogue)

(TOP RIGHT)
Right-hander Ferguson Jenkins (1976–77). One of the top pitchers of his era, Jenkins's best years were behind him when he reached Boston.

(BOTTOM LEFT)
Mike Torrez (1978–82).
(Photograph by Nancy Hogue)

(BOTTOM RIGHT)
Don Zimmer, Red Sox manager from 1976 to 1980.

November brought some consolation when Jim Rice edged Guidry for the MVP Award. Rice had been devastating all year, leading with 46 home runs, 15 triples, 213 hits, 139 RBIs, .600 slugging average, and 406 total bases—the highest number of total bases in the league since Joe DiMaggio in 1937.

Eckersley was 20–8, and Bob Stanley emerged as a bullpen ace with a 15–2 record. The Red Sox outscored the Yankees 796–735 and outhomered them 172–125. The difference lay in the 25–3 record put up by Guidry.

Rubbing a bit of salt in Boston's wounds, the Yankees in November wooed away the colorful and popular Tiant, who had become a free agent. Only two pitchers in Red Sox history, Cy Young and Mel Parnell, had more victories than Tiant's 122.

In 1979, the Sox received some healthy hitting from Lynn and Rice—39 home runs apiece and a .333 batting crown for Freddie—but finished third. Boston set a new club record with 310 doubles, and with 194 home runs was an exciting team to watch, and a new Fenway-record 2,353,114 came out to do just that.

Playing in a division acknowledged to be the strongest in baseball, a hard-hitting Red Sox team could do no better than fourth in 1980, and at the end of the season Zimmer was fired. The little round man had done well in Boston, winning 411 and losing 305, but still had no pennant to show for this excellent record. The hiring and firing of managers is often an arcane act. For Zimmer, a manager with an enviable winning percentage, one of the problems was his growing unpopularity with the fans, who were able to voice their disapproval through the forums offered by that fairly recent phenomenon, the call-in sports talk show, over which a man could be put through the wringer and hung out to dry. So Zimmer was gone, replaced by Ralph Houk, former skipper of the Yankees and Tigers, whom the club lured out of retirement.

Wherever he managed, Houk had the respect of his players, because he always fought for them and backed them to the hilt, and because he himself was a rather rugged character. He was called by some members of the press "the Major," the nickname going back to his World War II service (some of it pretty hot) with the Rangers. Houk was also known for his optimism, and this attractive trait was put to the test well before the start of the 1981 season.

Rick Burleson and Fred Lynn were soon to become free agents, and the Red Sox had doubts about being able to sign either one of them. So, rather than get nothing in return for these star players, trades were arranged. Burleson, along with Butch Hobson, went west to California in exchange for relief pitcher Mark Clear, third baseman Carney Lansford, and outfielder Rick Miller, who had originally come to the majors with Boston. A few weeks later Lynn was also dealt to the Angels, along with pitcher Steve Renko, for left-hander Frank Tanana and outfielder Joe Rudi—the same Rudi the Sox had tried to buy for $1 million just a few years before (but the same Rudi in name only; this once outstanding outfielder was just about through).

(LEFT)
Veteran southpaw Frank Tanana put in one season for the Red Sox—1981—and it was a disappointing one: he was 4–10.
(Photograph by Nancy Hogue)

(RIGHT)
Tom Burgmeier (1978–82). He appeared in 213 games for the Red Sox, 212 of them as a reliever.
(Photograph by Nancy Hogue)

That's Jerry Remy being nipped at second by Cleveland's Tom Veryzer. Remy, who played for Boston from 1978 to 1984, had his career cut short by a knee injury. *(Photograph by Nancy Hogue)*

Another top name from the 1970s clubs also departed at this time. Because of a clerical foul-up, the contract of Carlton Fisk was mailed too late. This constituted a breach of the rules and entitled him to free agency. (The same thing had happened with Lynn, but Boston traded him before he became a free agent.) Fisk put himself on the open market and signed with the White Sox.

So the Red Sox entered the 1981 season with young Rich Gedman behind the plate and Glenn Hoffman at short, with Miller replacing Lynn in center. It turned out to be the most bizarre season in major-league history. In mid-June, the players went on strike, and baseball shut down for what would be a full third of the schedule. The meetings, rumors, and negotiations went on until an agreement was reached and play resumed in early August.

At this point, it was decided to decree 1981 a split season. The teams in first place when the strike began were declared the first-half winners. In the American League East, this was New

York (Boston was fourth). The second-half winner was Milwaukee, with Boston finishing just one and a half games out, thus depriving Houk's club of a shot at the Yankees for the division title.

Again Boston had to be satisfied with some individual achievements. Lansford provided the team with yet another batting champion, the third baseman compiling a .336 average, while Evans tied for the home-run lead with 22. The Sox also found they had a fine young catcher in Gedman, who batted .288.

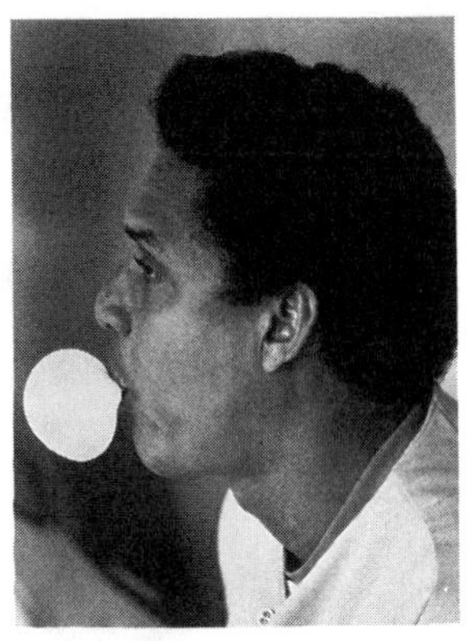

Tony Perez (1980–82). Between bubbles the former Cincinnati star drove in 105 runs for the Sox in 1980.
(Photograph by Nancy Hogue)

The 1982 season started well for Houk's men, thanks in part to a well-stocked bullpen that included Clear, Stanley, and left-hander Tom Burgmeier. The Red Sox were in the thick of things until July, but then a lack of solid starting pitching gradually worked them into a third-place finish, six games behind Milwaukee, who won the division by beating second-place Baltimore on the last day of the season.

Evans turned in a solid season with 32 home runs and a .292 average, while Rice maintained the Fenway left-field tradition—begun by Williams and carried on by Yastrzemski—by hitting 24 homers and batting .309.

The most significant addition to the Red Sox lineup in 1982 came about because of an injury to Lansford. With the third baseman down, Houk inserted into the lineup twenty-four-year-old rookie Wade Boggs. A left-handed hitter with a stroke that took full advantage of the accommodating wall in left field, Boggs had been waiting for his chance. (The farseeing youngster had signed with Boston because he knew the Wall was tailor-made to receive his high, slicing fly balls and line drives.) The man who was to become the premier high-average hitter of his era, and one of the greatest of all time, launched his career with a .349 average, though without sufficient plate appearances to qualify for the batting title.

Boggs divided his time between third base and first, but his debut was impressive enough for the Sox to trade Lansford

(TOP LEFT)
Shortstop Glenn Hoffman (1980–87).

(TOP RIGHT)
Boston second baseman Dave Stapleton has just forced Baltimore's Al Bumbry at second and is firing to first to complete the double play. Stapleton (1980–86) batted .321 in his rookie year, but never repeated that success.

(BOTTOM LEFT)
Bob Stanley.
(Photograph by Nancy Hogue)

(BOTTOM RIGHT)
Ralph Houk in a familiar dugout pose. He managed the Red Sox from 1981 through 1984.
(Photograph by Nancy Hogue)

after the season. Carney went to Oakland in exchange for right-handed power-hitting outfielder Tony Armas.

In 1983, despite some lusty individual performances, Boston dropped to sixth place, the club's worst showing since a ninth-place finish in 1966. Houk had three talented left-handers at the top of his staff in John Tudor (13–12), Bob Ojeda (12–7), and Bruce Hurst (12–12), but Eckersley fell to 9–13.

The free-swinging Armas hit 36 home runs and drove in 107 runs but batted just .218. Rice led the league with 39 homers, had 126 RBIs, and batted .305. The glory of Boston this year was Wade Boggs, who took the first of his many batting crowns with a .361 average, bolstered by 210 hits, including 44 doubles, many of them "wall balls."

"This guy," one exasperated but admiring American League pitcher said of Boggs, "is going to be a first-class nuisance for a long time."

The season ended on a nostalgic note of farewell. After twenty-three years, Carl Yastrzemski was retiring. To those for whom baseball seasons telescoped one into the other as smoothly as ocean waves, it hardly seemed almost a quarter century since the twenty-one-year-old youngster had moved into left field to replace Williams. Those who doubted that the calendar could be correct had only to look at the record book to see that more than two decades had indeed transpired, for there it all lay, the days and works of Carl Yastrzemski, embroidered in statistics that in their sum total recorded one of the longest and most successful careers in baseball history. And among this abundance was a distinction that belonged to Yastrzemski alone: the only man in American League history to amass more than 400 home runs (452) and more than 3,000 hits (3,419).

Yastrzemski's farewell to Fenway was a sentimental pregame tour of the field. The old park seemed to turn heart-shaped as the veteran circled it for the last time as an active player, trotting and waving and touching the hands of those who reached out. It was indeed rare for a player to have spent an

(LEFT)
Carney Lansford (1981–82).
(Photograph by Nancy Hogue)

(RIGHT)
Rick Miller (1971–77, 1981–85). A superb defensive outfielder, Miller was in his later years Boston's top pinch hitter.
(Photograph by Nancy Hogue)

entire twenty-three-year career with a single club; in the age of free agency, such players may now be a vanished species.

Yastrzemski's retirement had immediate impact on the Red Sox. Feeling the need for a left-handed bat to replace him, Boston traded John Tudor to Pittsburgh for Mike Easler, basically a DH. Early in the 1984 season, the Sox added another left-handed bat to the lineup when they traded Eckersley to the Chicago Cubs for veteran first baseman Bill Buckner. Another addition to the regular alignment was second baseman Marty Barrett, a product of the farm system.

The 1984 Red Sox were a hard-hitting team, with Boggs at .325 (and 203 hits), Easler at .313, Barrett at .303. Armas led the league with 43 home runs and 123 RBIs, giving the club its sixteenth home-run leader in its history (only the Yankees have had more). The team blasted 181 home runs and had five men with more than twenty: Armas; Evans, 32; Rice, 28; Easler, 27; and Gedman, 24.

Dwight Evans, Boston's rocket-armed right fielder.
(Photograph by Nancy Hogue)

Despite this potent offense, Boston finished fourth, eighteen games behind a Detroit team that won thirty-five of its first forty and then ran away and hid. Boston's top winners were Hurst, Ojeda, and newcomer Dennis ("Oil Can") Boyd, each with a 12–12 record.

There was another newcomer to the staff—twenty-one-year-old right-hander Roger Clemens, whom the team had been grooming for stardom ever since drafting him out of the University of Texas the year before. Clemens pitched briefly in the minors in 1983, then started the 1984 season with Boston's top farm club at Pawtucket, Rhode Island. By May, the sizzle of the husky youngster's ninety-five-mile-an-hour fastball was an irresistible call, and he was brought up to the big club.

Carl Yastrzemski is looking deep.
(Photograph by Ronald C. Modra)

"If he's as good as we think he is," one club official said, "then we're in clover."

"And how good do you think he is?" someone asked.

The official thought it over for a moment. "He could be the best pitcher we've had here since Joe Wood."

On the wings of that grand pronouncement, Clemens put up a 9–4 record with 126 strikeouts in 133 innings before an arm injury ended his season in late August.

The club had a new manager in 1985, Houk having resigned. The Major left the big-league managerial ranks with a rare distinction—he had never been fired, voluntarily leaving

Mark Clear (1981–85). *(Photograph by Nancy Hogue)*

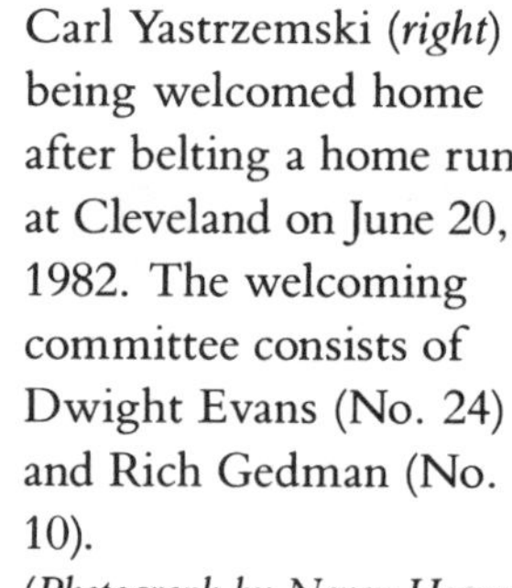

Carl Yastrzemski (*right*) being welcomed home after belting a home run at Cleveland on June 20, 1982. The welcoming committee consists of Dwight Evans (No. 24) and Rich Gedman (No. 10). *(Photograph by Nancy Hogue)*

(TOP LEFT)
Tony Armas (1983–86). His 43 home runs and 123 RBIs led the league in 1984.

(TOP RIGHT)
Rich Gedman.
(Courtesy TV Sports Mailbag)

(BOTTOM LEFT)
Wade Boggs, the base-hit-factory.

(BOTTOM RIGHT)
Jim Rice.
(Photograph by Nancy Hogue)

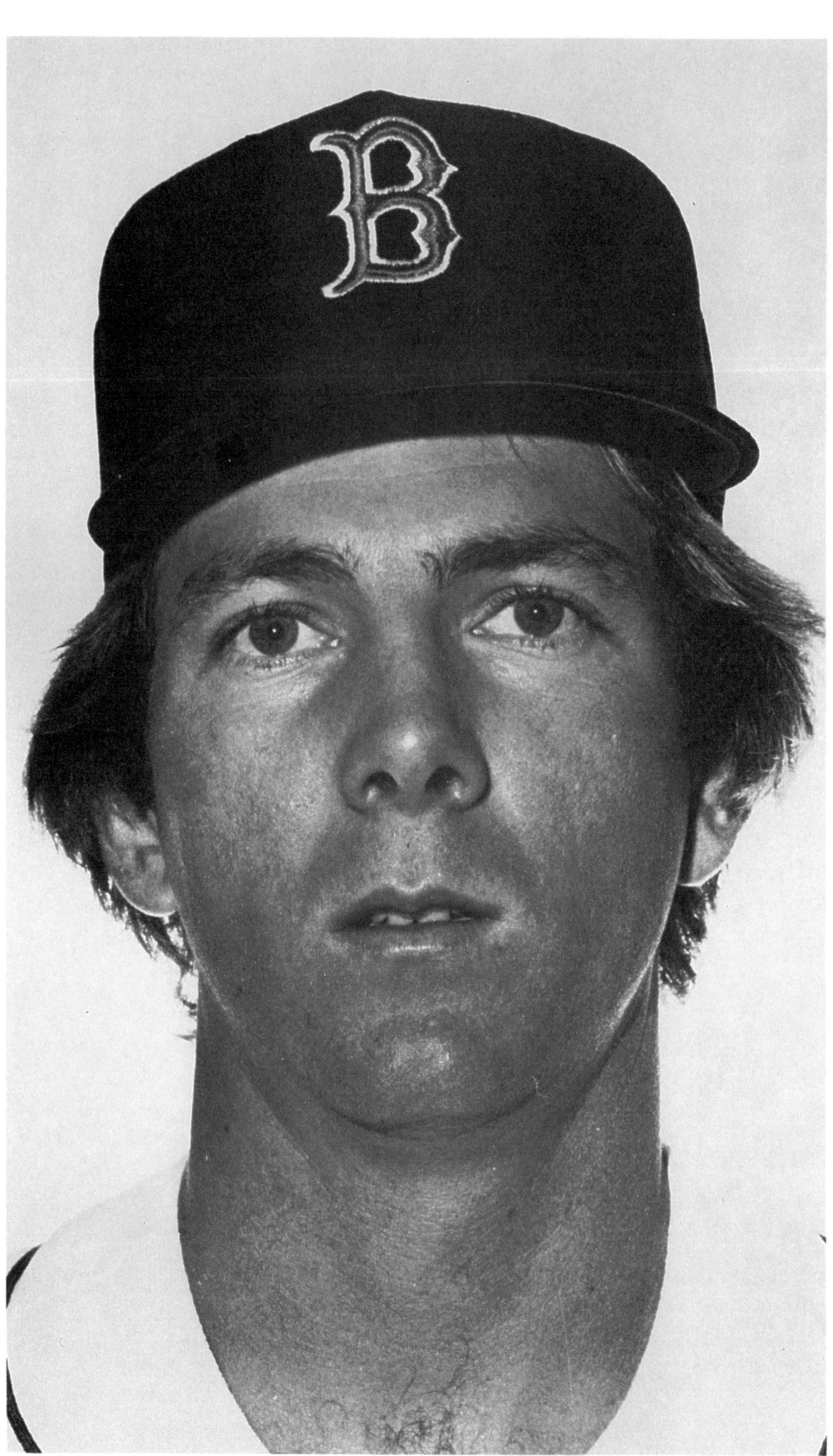

John Tudor (1979–83).

(LEFT)
Mike Easler (1984–85).

(RIGHT)
Al Nipper (1983–87), who had the knack—much appreciated in New England—of beating the Yankees.

his positions with the Yankees, the Tigers, and now the Red Sox.

The new skipper was John McNamara, a product of baseball's old-boy network of managers. Before coming to Boston, McNamara, who never played in the majors but had spent fourteen years as a catcher in the minors, managed at Oakland, San Diego, Cincinnati, and California, with his best effort a division title with the Reds in 1979.

"Johnny Mac" had a disappointing first year in Boston in 1985, finishing fifth, despite a team batting average of .282, by far the league's highest. The biggest contributor to this figure was Wade Boggs, taking his second batting championship with a .368 mark, achieved by means of 240 hits, most ever by a Red Sox player. Among this truckload of hits were 187 singles, a new American League record. Boggs was the club's only .300 hitter, though Buckner, Rice, and Gedman were in the .290s.

Boyd led the staff with 15 wins, while the man everyone was looking to, Clemens, was held to a 7–5 record in a season riddled with shoulder miseries. On August 30, the young fireballer underwent arthroscopic surgery on the troublesome shoulder, which automatically labeled him a question mark for the coming season. This led the historically minded among Red Sox fans to begin wondering about the "jinx" that afflicted their star right-handers. They thought about Joe Wood, Tex Hughson, Dave Ferriss, Jim Lonborg—ace pitchers all, who had seen one injury or another close their Fenway careers before high noon. But in the case of Roger Clemens, they need not have worried.

— 12 —

Another Pennant

SOX

The 1986 season was one of the most memorable in Red Sox history. It was a summer of unexpected delights and then a postseason that included a miracle comeback and a devastating disappointment. For Boston, it was a scrapbook of baseball at its mightiest, its most dramatically entertaining, and its most heartbreaking.

After their fifth-place finish in 1985, the Red Sox were not expected to contend in 1986. Most experts picked them for another deep spot in the standings. The forecast was forgivable, because no one could possibly have foreseen that Roger Clemens would burn through the league like a blowtorch.

The greatness that the Red Sox had suspected lay within Clemens suddenly was upon them in full blast. Pampered during spring training because of his recent shoulder surgery, Roger (soon to be known as "the Rocket Man") was out of the gate like a sprinter in a mile-long race, winning his first fourteen decisions. Victory number 4, against Seattle at Fenway on April 29, was a landmark in the annals of pitching. In shutting down the Mariners, 3–1, Clemens made headlines by striking out twenty batters, establishing a new one-game record, exceeding by one the previous mark that had been held jointly by Steve Carlton, Nolan Ryan, and Tom Seaver.

Along with Clemens, who finished the season with a 24–4 record, the Sox had Boyd at 16–10 and Hurst (who lost some time to injuries) at 13–8. The club also got good pitching from midseason acquisition Seaver, who finished out his sparkling career with the Sox, going 5–7. (A late-season knee injury kept him out of the postseason games.) Manning the bullpen were Bob Stanley and, later in the season, right-hander Calvin Schiraldi. Schiraldi and righty Wes Gardner (lost all year because of a sore arm) had come to the Red Sox in a swap with the Mets that saw Bob Ojeda go to New York.

Boggs won his third batting title, with a .357 average, drilling 207 hits. Rice batted .324, drove in 110 runs, and had

(OPPOSITE PAGE)
John McNamara, Boston manager from 1985 through July of 1988.

(TOP LEFT)
Marty Barrett.

(TOP RIGHT)
Don Baylor (1986–87).

(BOTTOM LEFT)
Bill Buckner (1984–87). He twice drove in more than 100 runs for the Red Sox, but that's not what he'll be remembered for.

(BOTTOM RIGHT)
Wade Boggs.

200 hits. Don Baylor, acquired from the Yankees in exchange for Mike Easler, was the club's DH most of the year and hit 31 homers and drove in 94 runs despite a .238 average. Buckner had 102 RBIs, while Evans hit 26 homers and had 97 RBIs. Late in the season, GM Lou Gorman made a trade with Seattle, sending shortstop Ray Quinones to the West Coast for shortstop Spike Owen and utility outfielder Dave Henderson, a trade that would have historic resonance for Boston. The regular lineup was rounded out by Armas, Gedman, and Barrett (who had 15 of the club's 41 stolen bases).

Ed Romero, Boston's invaluable utility man.

McNamara's men took over sole possession of first place on May 15 and thereafter defended it against charges by New York, Detroit, and Toronto. The biggest outburst of the year came at Cleveland on August 21, when the Sox took apart the Indians by a 24–5 score on a twenty-four-hit attack. Owen tied a major-league record by scoring six runs. (The only other American Leaguer to score six times in a game was another Boston shortstop—Johnny Pesky, in 1946.)

Spike Owen (1986–88).

When the Red Sox went 3–10 after the All-Star break, the cynics began winking at each other, looking for a Boston collapse. But the club restored itself in August, and an eleven-game winning streak from August 30 to September 10 all but locked up the division title. The final margin was five and a half games over the Yankees.

Awaiting Boston in the League Championship Series (now a best-of-seven affair) were Gene Mauch's California Angels, a club buttressed by some strong starting pitching in Mike Witt, Kirk McCaskill, Don Sutton, and John Candelaria.

The series opened in Boston with Witt beating Clemens, 8–1. Hurst, always a money pitcher, evened it the next day with a 9–2 win.

Marc Sullivan (1982, 1984–87).

In California, Candelaria beat Boyd 5–3 in the third game. The following night, the Angels took a formidable three-games-to-one edge with a 4–3, eleven-inning victory, after

Roger Clemens: back-to-back Cy Young Awards.

having tied it with a three-run bottom of the ninth. This disheartening defeat seemed to seal Boston's fate, but this was a Red Sox club with some kick in it.

The fifth game of the series remains one of the most memorable in postseason annals. Trailing 5–2 going into the top of the ninth, the Red Sox seemed doomed. But then Baylor hit a two-run homer and, with two out, Dave Henderson etched his name in Red Sox history by blasting another two-run shot, putting the Sox a run up. The Angels tied it in the last of the ninth and had the bases loaded with two out, but reliever Steve Crawford, in a gutty exhibition of derring-do, wriggled off the hook. In the top of the eleventh, a sacrifice fly by Henderson sent across what would be the winning run in a remarkable 7–6 victory. Ironically, the only reason Henderson was playing was because of an injury suffered by Armas earlier in the game. (His big home run was the only hit Henderson had in nine at-bats in the series.)

Back in Fenway, the reprieved Red Sox rolled to a pair of easy 10–4 and 8–1 victories behind Boyd and Clemens, giving the club its first pennant since 1975. After having been edged out of pennants by excruciatingly narrow margins in 1948, 1949, 1972, and 1978, Boston had finally taken a close one.

Bruce Hurst (1980–88), who left for San Diego gold.

Right-hander Steve Crawford (1980–82, 1984–87).

The scene from deep right field. (*Courtesy NBL*)

Was Dave Henderson's home run the biggest single hit in Red Sox history? Bigger than Fisk's dramatic homer in Game 6 of the 1975 World Series? The answer has to be "yes." While Fisk's shot had all the impact of winning an emotion-drenched World Series game, it was a tie-breaking shot, lacking the do-or-die momentousness of Henderson's. Without Henderson's home run, Boston's season would have been over, right then and there. It was the dynamite clutch hit Boston fans had been waiting for since 1948. (Not to be overlooked, however, is Carbo's game-tying pinch-hit home run in that famous sixth game in 1975.)

Calvin Schiraldi (1986–87).

The National League champion New York Mets had played a thrilling LCS themselves, winning the pennant in a sixteen-inning "everything included" game with the Houston Astros. The general feeling among baseball people was that after these gripping battles for the respective pennants, the World Series would be anticlimactic. The Mets and Red Sox, however, still had some theater left in them and would produce a game to match anything that had gone before.

(Left)
Tom Seaver, who finished out his illustrious big-league career with Boston in 1986. A knee injury prevented his participation in postseason play.

(Right)
Dave Henderson (1986–87). Probably the single most momentous home run in Red Sox history.

It's the top of the seventh inning of Game 4 of the 1986 World Series. Dwight Evans is making a heroic attempt to bring in Lenny Dykstra's drive to right field, but the ball has popped out of his glove and is going for a home run.

The Series opened at New York's Shea Stadium with Hurst, getting a ninth-inning hand from Schiraldi, nipping the Mets' Ron Darling, 1–0. Boston then made it two in a row with a 9–3 thrashing of Dwight Gooden.

The focus then shifted to Fenway, with Red Sox fans entertaining a pair of giddy notions: a four-game sweep, or, at the very least, the club's first world championship since 1918.

The Mets, however, came bounding back. They dispelled all ideas of a sweep by ambushing Boyd in a four-run first inning and going on to win, 7–1, behind a man who was no stranger to Fenway, Bob Ojeda. The Mets tied the Series the following night, Darling beating Al Nipper, 6–2. Boston then took a three-games-to-two advantage when Hurst beat Gooden, 4–2.

Jim Rice is being tagged out at home by the Mets' Gary Carter in the top of the seventh inning of Game 6 of the 1986 World Series. The umpire is Dale Ford.

The sixth game of the 1986 Series not only ended on a bizarre note, it also began with one. In the top of the first inning a parachutist made an unscheduled landing in the infield. He was quickly taken into custody. Catcher Gary Carter, plate umpire Dale Ford, and Red Sox batter Bill Buckner (No. 6) are among the bemused spectators.

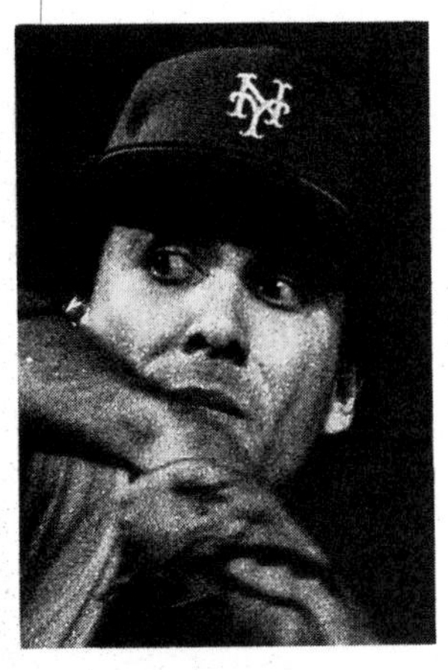

Former Boston left-hander Bob Ojeda working against his former teammates in the 1986 World Series. Ojeda pitched for the Red Sox from 1980 to 1985.

Thus far it had been a fairly routine World Series, the ball bouncing according to the precepts laid down by Abner Doubleday a hundred and fifty years ago. But now came Game 6, an affair to be remembered, or, depending on your perspective, forgotten.

Boston started off well, scoring runs in the first and second innings against Ojeda, while Clemens was firing blazers. At the end of four innings it was still 2–0, with Clemens pitching hitless ball. In the last of the fifth, the Mets scored twice to tie it. In the top of the seventh the Sox went up 3–2, on an unearned run. Clemens left after the seventh with a blister on his finger. The Mets quickly tied it at 3–3 against Schiraldi.

The tie lasted until the top of the tenth, at which point Dave Henderson hit one out to put the Sox up, 4–3. Boston scored another run and went into the last of the tenth with a two-run lead and three outs to get.

Schiraldi got the first out, then the second. Then came three straight singles, by Gary Carter, Kevin Mitchell, and Ray Knight, making it 5–4, two out and Mitchell on third, 55,000 fans on their feet, and the Mets and Red Sox on the edges of their respective dugouts.

McNamara went to the mound, removed Schiraldi and brought in the veteran Stanley to face switch-hitter Mookie Wilson. The count went to 2–2. Wilson fouled off the next two pitches. Stanley then delivered a pitch that seemed to take on a life of its own. "It was an inside fastball," an unhappy Stanley said later, "that was supposed to tail back out over the plate." Instead, the ball tailed sharply in and down on Wilson, who leaped into the air and seemed to hang suspended for a moment while Gedman dived to his right to try and catch the errant delivery. The ball got by him and went all the way to the screen while Mitchell roared home with the tying run and Knight went to second.

After fouling off two more pitches, Wilson hit a three-bouncer down to first baseman Bill Buckner, a Series subhero for playing on tired and battered ankles. Buckner waited for that last bounce, but it was a slightly erratic one, going under his glove and into short right field as Knight tore around third and came in with the winning run.

The rally that couldn't and shouldn't have happened *had* happened, and now Game 7 loomed—for Boston, its fourth consecutive full-length World Series, following those in 1946, 1967, and 1975.

After a day's respite because of rain, Hurst went to the mound for Boston and Darling for New York. Behind home runs by Evans and Gedman and a run-scoring hit by Boggs, Boston took a 3–0 lead after three innings (precisely the situation after three innings in Game 7 against the Reds in 1975, a fact noted by some New England fatalists).

The Mets tied it in the last of the sixth, then took a 6–3 lead with three more in the seventh. Boston fought back to 6–5 in the top of the eighth, but the Mets iced it with two in the

It has just happened: Mookie Wilson's grounder has just passed through the Buckner wickets. Bob Stanley (No. 46) has run over to cover first. On the right are umpire Jim Evans and Mets' first-base coach Bill Robinson.

bottom of the eighth and went on to an 8–5 victory and the world championship.

Marty Barrett gave the Red Sox a standout performance in defeat, tying a Series record with thirteen hits (after rapping out eleven in the LCS against California).

But it was Game 6 that will always characterize the 1986 World Series, and for Red Sox fans the haunting thoughts were the blister that removed Clemens from the game, the Stanley wild pitch, the Buckner error. Solace, however, could be taken from the philosophy of longtime big-league manager Chuck Tanner, who once said, "The greatest thing in baseball is winning the World Series. The second greatest is losing the World Series." In other words, Boston—and not thirteen other American League teams—had been there.

In the fall, Clemens was rewarded for his magnificent season by winning both the Most Valuable Player and Cy Young awards.

There were ominous shadows for the 1987 season, even before a pitch was thrown. Clemens walked out of the club's spring camp because of a contract dispute and did not return until April 4. Boyd developed shoulder problems before the season opened and was limited to just seven appearances all year. Another contract dispute kept Gedman out of the lineup until early May, and between rustiness and injuries the husky catcher never did get untracked, batting just .205.

Sluggish play had the defending American League champions out of the race by mid-June. At that point, the club decided to make practical use of the rest of the season by giving some of their younger players an opportunity to play. This meant the departure of a few veterans: Bill Buckner was released, Don Baylor was traded to Minnesota, and Dave Henderson was swapped to the San Francisco Giants. This opened the way for Mike Greenwell, Ellis Burks, and Todd Benzinger, and these eager, talented youngsters took full advantage of their opportunities. Greenwell batted .328, hit 19 home runs, and drove in 89 runs in just 412 at-bats. Burks batted .272 and gave Boston some excellent play in center field, in addition to stealing 27 bases, most by a Red Sox player since Jerry Remy's 30 in 1978. The switch-hitting Benzinger batted .276.

Among the veterans, Evans seemed to be getting better, putting together career highs with a .305 batting average, 34 home runs, and 123 RBIs. For Boggs, it was another routine year—his third straight batting title and fourth overall with a .363 average and 200 hits. With this latter figure, Boggs entered a particularly elite group, joining Hall of Famers Chuck Klein, Al Simmons, and Charlie Gehringer as the only men to rack up 200 or more hits for five consecutive seasons.

Despite his slow start—he was 6–6 at the end of June—Clemens went on to a 20–9 record, winning his twentieth game on the final day of the season. He had 256 strikeouts, led the league with seven shutouts, and after the season was voted his second straight Cy Young Award.

(Left)
Todd Benzinger (1987–88).
(Courtesy TV Sports Mailbag)

(Right)
Roger Clemens. He was unstoppable in 1986.
(Courtesy TV Sports Mailbag)

As far as some people were concerned, the Red Sox became serious contenders for 1988 on December 8, 1987, for that was the day they obtained Lee Smith from the Chicago Cubs. The thirty-year-old Smith had for a half-dozen years been one of baseball's top relief pitchers. The 6′6″, 245-pound right-hander with the blazing fastball had notched more than thirty saves for four years in a row. He was exactly the type of bullpen force the Red Sox had been lacking. Some people felt that Smith was going to be the most intimidating Red Sox reliever since Radatz.

Wes Gardner.

In order to pry Smith away from the Cubs, Lou Gorman had to part with right-handers Al Nipper and Calvin Schiraldi. Always a willing worker and something of a Yankee killer, Nipper had proved to be little better than a .500 pitcher for Boston, while Schiraldi had not been the stopper the Sox had hoped he would be.

With Smith in the pen to back up Clemens, Hurst, and the other starters, the Sox went into the 1988 season with high

(Left)
Mike Greenwell, who picked up the left field tradition of stardom.

(Right)
Wade Boggs.
(Courtesy TV Sports Mailbag)

expectations. The club, however, was sluggish and inconsistent throughout the first half, getting to the All-Star break with a 43–42 record, in fourth place, nine games out. For several weeks, rumors had been circulating that McNamara's job was in jeopardy. A 4–8 road trip prior to the break sealed the skipper's fate.

On July 14, as the schedule resumed after the All-Star interlude, it was announced that McNamara had been fired. His successor was third-base coach Joe Morgan. The fifty-seven-year-old Morgan (known in the trade as "the other Joe Morgan," in deference to the former great National League second baseman) had had a brief major-league career, during which he played for Milwaukee, Kansas City, Philadelphia, Cleveland, and St. Louis, getting into just eighty-eight games and batting a modest .193. Later came a sixteen-year minor-league managerial career. And now the native of nearby Walpole was running the big team, at least to the end of the season.

Morgan's first moves as he took over the club were to switch the positions of right fielder Todd Benzinger and first baseman Dwight Evans and to install Jody Reed at shortstop in place of Spike Owen. What happened after that can only be reported, not explained.

Kansas City came to Fenway for a four-game series and was swept. Boston was now six games behind. Minnesota came in for three and was swept. Chicago came in for four and was swept. Boston was now one and a half back. The Sox added another to their string at Texas before absorbing their first loss under Morgan after twelve straight wins. The phrase "Morgan Magic" was now part of New England's baseball vocabulary.

At the end of July, Lou Gorman made a fine deal when he acquired Baltimore right-hander Mike Boddicker in exchange for young outfielder Brady Anderson. With Boddicker supplementing starters Clemens, Hurst, and Gardner, the club continued winning.

(TOP LEFT)
Rich Gedman.

(TOP RIGHT)
Marty Barrett.

(BOTTOM LEFT)
Jody Reed.
(Courtesy TV Sports Mailbag)

(BOTTOM RIGHT)
Nick Esasky.

(TOP LEFT)
Ed Romero.

(TOP RIGHT)
Sam Horn.

(BOTTOM LEFT)
Jim Rice.
(Courtesy TV Sports Mailbag)

(BOTTOM RIGHT)
Ellis Burks.

Unbeatable at home, the Sox stubbed their toes on a trip to Detroit in the beginning of August. After losing the first four games of a five-game set at Tiger Stadium, it looked as if "Morgan Magic" was wearing off. But in the finale, in what Morgan was later to call the season's key game, Hurst pitched a ten-inning, 3–0 victory to get the team turned around.

Returning to Fenway, the team scored a league-record twenty-fourth consecutive home victory on August 12. (Morgan was soon signed to manage the club in 1989.)

On September 4, Boston and Detroit were tied for first place with identical 75–61 records, with New York and Milwaukee each four games out. At this point, Detroit began to slide away and New York continued to hang close.

On September 15, the Yankees came to Fenway to begin a pair of home-and-home weekend series, four games in Boston and then three in New York. As New York arrived in town, they were four and a half behind Boston. Those with long memories recalled New York's four-game visit to Fenway in September 1978, when the Yankees swept the Sox and tied them for first place. To a lot of Boston fans, this old nightmare became slightly more vivid when New York took the opener, 5–3. The next night, however, Gardner, with the help of Smith, pushed the Yankees back by a 7–4 score. The Sox then went on to delight their fans with 3–1 and 9–4 victories in the next two games.

When Boston arrived in New York for the three-game series there, the lead over the Yankees was back to four and a half. On Friday night, September 23, the Sox won the game that broke the backs and hearts of New York. Trailing 9–7 going into the ninth, Boston mounted a three-run rally and took a 10–9 lead that Smith protected. The clubs split the final two games, and Boston went into the season's final week four and a half games over Detroit, five over Milwaukee, and five and a half over New York.

(TOP LEFT)
Dwight Evans.

(TOP RIGHT)
Mike Boddicker.
(Courtesy TV Sports Mailbag)

(BOTTOM LEFT)
Rick Cerone.

(BOTTOM RIGHT)
Mike Smithson.

There was some stumbling around in the final week, but Boston finally clinched the division on September 30, when Milwaukee and New York eliminated themselves with losses. Boston's final margin was a single game over Detroit.

The two grueling series with the Yankees seemed to have taken something out of the Red Sox, who went on to lose six of their last seven regular-season games. From there they went on to the League Championship Series against a powerful Oakland club and never won a game.

The series opened in Boston with a 2–1 Athletics victory. Performing some postseason heroics once more, this time for Oakland, was Dave Henderson, whose eighth-inning single drove in the deciding run. Oakland took the second game by another narrow margin, 4–3. Boston lost an early 5–0 lead in the third game and wound up down by a 10–6 score. It all came to an end the next day with a 4–1 Oakland pennant-clincher.

So instead of their eleventh pennant, Boston had to go into the winter content with a division title, the third they had taken since divisional play began in 1969.

For Wade Boggs, it was another year of exceptional achievement. The third baseman took his fifth batting title and fourth in a row with a .366 batting average (it was Boston's twenty-first batting title) and, with 214 hits, became the first man in history to accumulate 200 or more hits six years in a row. The Boston clockwork hitter also led in runs (128), walks (125), and doubles (45) and had an on-base percentage of .476, 60 points higher than the next man, teammate Mike Greenwell.

Greenwell put together the kind of year that had him being talked about as a potential MVP through much of the summer. (The vote eventually went to Oakland's Jose Canseco.) Greenwell batted .325, with 22 home runs, and 119 RBIs. With this new young star now the regular left fielder, it was apparent that that position's tradition of excellence, begun with Williams and carried on through Yastrzemski and Rice, was going to continue.

Reed, vindicating the faith Morgan had placed in him, batted .293, the same as Evans and a point under Burks. This was a good-hitting Red Sox team, with a collective batting average of .283, tops in the league.

Clemens finished at 18–12, with shoulder trouble costing him a chance for a third straight twenty-victory season (as well as a crack at what would have been a record-setting third straight Cy Young Award). Roger had enough sizzle, however, to amass 291 strikeouts, which led the league and also broke Joe Wood's club mark of 258, set in 1912.

Hurst put together his best year, with an 18–6 ledger. The fine left-hander was now a free agent, and that superb won-lost figure started blinking on and off like a garish neon light, attracting multimillion-dollar offers. Although Boston's offer was more than competitive, Hurst finally opted for the San Diego Padres, leaving a considerable gap in Boston's pitching staff.

(LEFT) Dennis ("Oil Can") Boyd.

(RIGHT) Lee Smith.

Joe Morgan.

(Left)
Boston Red Sox general manager Lou Gorman.

(Right)
Jean Yawkey.

Haywood Sullivan.

Smith had been everything the Sox had hoped he would be. Playing baseball's cavalry role, the big, hard-throwing reliever had saved 29 games and had proved to be the club's key link in its successful quest for a division title.

Lou Gorman's most significant postseason activity in 1988 was a four-man trade with Cincinnati. Leaving Boston were Todd Benzinger and young right-hander Jeff Sellers; coming east were power-hitting infielder Nick Esasky and left-handed reliever Rob Murphy.

And so the uniforms and the bats and the balls were packed away once more, and Fenway's gates were closed to await the passage of winter, to see through the time of snow on the field's green grass and in the grandstands and bleachers. And once more the team scattered to their homes across the country, leaving behind another summer of history recorded in the enchanting old ball park just off Kenmore Square.

The winter snow piling up in the Fenway Park grandstand.

Whoever plays at Fenway now has generations of history at his back, and whatever is no longer vivid in living memory is secure in the record books, those telltale chronicles of all that has gone before: from Cy Young and Smoky Joe to Speaker and the Babe, from Cronin and Grove and Foxx to Williams and Yastrzemski, to Rice and Clemens and Boggs, and to all the shareholders of that history, on the field and in the stands.

The close of one season is always fragrant with the promise of the next. A baseball fan marks his calendar: Thanksgiving, Christmas, New Year's, and then thoughts can reasonably turn once again to baseball, and spring training, and Opening Day, and another long, sweet run through summer, toward the alluring dividends of October, baseball's own time of festivity.

— Appendix —

Red Sox League Leaders

HOME RUNS

1903	Freeman	13
1910	Stahl	10
1912	Speaker	10
1918	Ruth	11
1919	Ruth	29
1939	Foxx	35
1941	Williams	37
1942	Williams	36
1947	Williams	32
1949	Williams	43
1965	Conigliaro	32
1967	Yastrzemski	44
1977	Rice	39
1978	Rice	46
1981	Evans	22
1983	Rice	39
1984	Armas	43

TRIPLES

1904	Stahl	22
1950	DiMaggio	11
	Doerr	11
1956	Jensen	11
1972	Fisk	9
1978	Rice	15

DOUBLES

1912	Speaker	53
1914	Speaker	46
1931	Webb	67
1938	Cronin	51
1948	Williams	44
1949	Williams	39
1956	Piersall	40
1963	Yastrzemski	40
1965	Yastrzemski	45
1966	Yastrzemski	39
1968	Smith	37
1971	Smith	33
1975	Lynn	47
1988	Boggs	45

HITS

1903	Dougherty	195
1914	Speaker	193
1938	Vosmik	201
1940	Cramer	200
1942	Pesky	205
1946	Pesky	208
1947	Pesky	207
1963	Yastrzemski	183
1967	Yastrzemski	189
1978	Rice	213
1985	Boggs	240

RUNS BATTED IN

1902	Freeman	121
1903	Freeman	104
1919	Ruth	114
1938	Foxx	175
1939	Williams	145
1942	Williams	137
1947	Williams	114
1949	Williams	159
	Stephens	159
1950	Stephens	144
	Dropo	144
1955	Jensen	116
1958	Jensen	122
1959	Jensen	112
1963	Stuart	118
1967	Yastrzemski	121
1968	Harrelson	109
1978	Rice	139
1983	Rice	126
1984	Armas	123

BATTING

1932	Alexander	.367
1938	Foxx	.349
1941	Williams	.406
1942	Williams	.356
1947	Williams	.343
1948	Williams	.369
1950	Goodman	.354
1957	Williams	.388
1958	Williams	.328
1960	Runnels	.320
1962	Runnels	.326
1963	Yastrzemski	.321
1967	Yastrzemski	.326
1968	Yastrzemski	.301
1979	Lynn	.333
1981	Lansford	.336
1983	Boggs	.361
1985	Boggs	.368
1986	Boggs	.357
1987	Boggs	.363
1988	Boggs	.366

WINS

1901	Young	33
1902	Young	32
1903	Young	28
1912	Wood	34
1935	Ferrell	25
1942	Hughson	22
1949	Parnell	25
1955	Sullivan	18
1967	Lonborg	22
1986	Clemens	24
1987	Clemens	20

STRIKEOUTS

1901	Young	158
1942	Hughson	113
1967	Lonborg	246
1988	Clemens	291

EARNED RUN AVERAGE

1901	Young	1.62
1914	Leonard	1.01
1915	Wood	1.49
1916	Ruth	1.75
1935	Grove	2.70
1936	Grove	2.81
1938	Grove	3.08
1939	Grove	2.54
1949	Parnell	2.77
1972	Tiant	1.91
1986	Clemens	2.48

INDEX

NOTE: Numbers in italics indicate photographs